Andrew Carnegie

Andrew Carnegie

An Economic Biography

Updated Edition

Samuel Bostaph

ROWMAN & LITTLEFIELD
Lanham • Boulder • New York • London

Published by Rowman & Littlefield
A wholly owned subsidiary of The Rowman & Littlefield Publishing Group, Inc.
4501 Forbes Boulevard, Suite 200, Lanham, Maryland 20706
www.rowman.com

Unit A, Whitacre Mews, 26-34 Stannary Street, London SE11 4AB

Distributed by NATIONAL BOOK NETWORK

British Library Cataloguing in Publication Information Available

Library of Congress Cataloging-in-Publication Data

Names: Bostaph, Samuel, author.
Title: Andrew Carnegie : an economic biography / Samuel Bostaph.
Description: Updated edition. | Lanham : Rowman & Littlefield, 2017. | Includes bibliographical references and index.
Identifiers: LCCN 2017020270 (print) | LCCN 2017029689 (ebook) | ISBN 9781538106006 (electronic) | ISBN 9781538100400 (pbk. : alk. paper)
Subjects: LCSH: Carnegie, Andrew, 1835–1919. | Industrialists—United States—Biography. | Philanthropists—United States—Biography. | Steel industry and trade—United States—History.
Classification: LCC CT275.C3 (ebook) | LCC CT275.C3 B67 2017 (print) | DDC 338.7672092 [B]—dc23
LC record available at https://lccn.loc.gov/2017020270

Printed in the United States of America

To my daughters, Katie and Megan, and to Maureen Tweedy

Contents

Preface   ix

Introduction   1

1 Entrepreneurial, Entrepreneurship, and Entrepreneurs   5

2 Early Life in Scotland   15

3 Youth in Western Pennsylvania   23

4 On the Road to Wealth   31

5 A Man of Steel   45

6 Labor Relations   73

7 Empire Builder   99

8 Philanthropist   121

9 A Summing Up   135

Notes   139

Bibliography   155

Index   159

About the Author   163

Preface

This biography of Andrew Carnegie is an "economic biography" in the same sense that Jonathan R. T. Hughes's fine study *The Vital Few: The Entrepreneur & American Economic Progress* (1965) can be described as a collection of economic biographies. Hughes presented the saga of ten entrepreneurial pioneers, including Carnegie, who were key figures in building the foundations of the American economy from the late seventeenth through the mid-twentieth centuries. His approach was to place each representative figure in his or her respective context and then relate how each contributed to the economic progress of that age. My ambition is both more modest and more specific. I restrict my story to that of one man and to the economic history of his rise from a poverty-stricken Scottish childhood to prominence as an international industrial leader, philanthropist, and peace advocate. I also treat him as an economic actor, whose alertness to profit opportunities and success in dealing with uncertainty in his profit-seeking efforts had both positive and negative effects for economic coordination in the U.S. and world market economies.

Like Hughes, I do not present Carnegie in all his detailed and multifaceted life, instead concentrating on his entrepreneurial role during the period when the United States was transformed from an agricultural and raw materials supplier into a manufacturing and industrial center. The three major historical biographies of Carnegie by Burton Hendrick (1932), Joseph Frazier Wall (1970), and David Nasaw (2006) are foundational to understanding Carnegie the man. Each in its own way is an excellent source of biographical detail. What this current book provides is an understanding of Carnegie as a dynamic entrepreneurial actor. It is that aspect of his existence in the burgeoning market economy of nineteenth-century America that has not previously received the emphasis it deserves.

Despite his many character flaws, Andrew Carnegie was arguably the most important entrepreneurial figure in the late nineteenth-century industrialization of the United States. In the following pages, I focus on his role as a driving force in the ascent of the United States to the position of premier manufacturing center of the world. It is also shown that he and his associates were sometimes agents of tremendous malinvestments, or even outright wastes of resources (which would have found other, more efficient channels of production for their usage than those to which they were actually put).

The world we inhabit is ruled by the physical laws given to us by nature, but it is also ruled by social laws that provide the context within which man employs nature to assist him in his purposeful actions. Physical laws are exact and constant in their causal implications, and man's physical being, as a part of nature, is governed by those laws. In addition, purposeful human actions reveal laws of rational choice, one category of which we term *economic laws*. Unlike physical laws, economic laws can be disregarded by acting man in choosing his ends and directing his actions; however, all actions have consequences, not all of which advance the ends chosen. It is no more possible to make a profit by selling a product at less than its resource opportunity cost than it is to sustain life while breathing in a vacuum. In addition, the political and cultural laws of society—the adopted rules that govern human interaction and create social institutions—are human constructs that may either aid or impede human flourishing, depending on their wisdom. Driven by his ambition, and acting within the political rules and the social institutions of his day, Andrew Carnegie pursued his own concepts of what was required for human flourishing as well as his own.

My thanks to Edward Younkins for suggesting that I send the original book proposal to Lexington Books; to Joseph C. Parry, Emily Roderick, and Sarah Craig for encouragement, support, and seeing the book through to press; to Jed Lyons for encouraging me to add new material to the original manuscript for an updated Rowman & Littlefield edition; and to Jonathan Sisk, Katelyn Powers, and Patricia Stevenson for reading, editing, and correcting the resulting trade paperback edition. From their efforts, it is much improved. I remain responsible for any remaining errors or omissions.

Introduction

In 1848, Andrew Carnegie was an impoverished and barely educated thirteen-year-old Scottish immigrant, whose first American job was bobbin boy in the Anchor Cotton Mill in Allegheny City, Pennsylvania. Although that city and Pittsburgh were separated by the Allegheny River, both were equally soot-drenched, thriving manufacturing and transportation centers. That thirteen-year-old boy worked twelve-hour days, six days a week, for which he was initially paid $1.20. Energetic, highly intelligent, and fueled by ambition, he went from bobbin boy to steam engine tender to accounts clerk to telegraph messenger boy within one year, his working conditions improving and his pay more than doubling as he rose. Assessing that period in his autobiography, Carnegie remarked, "There was scarcely a minute in which I could not learn something or find out how much there was to learn and how little I knew" (Carnegie, 1920, p. 39). As a result of this thirst for learning and his skillful use of it, in less than five years he had become the personal clerk and telegraph operator for Thomas A. Scott, the superintendent of the western Pennsylvania division of the Pennsylvania Railroad. By age seventeen, "Andy" Carnegie had his feet set firmly on the road to enormous wealth and legendary success in both business and philanthropy.

Standing a little more than five feet tall, with fair (later white) hair and blue eyes, Andrew Carnegie never used tobacco or foul language, drank alcohol moderately, and was a vocal opponent of slavery and of sexual discrimination in employment. He was generous to his friends and wore what little religion he had lightly. He was also an advocate of international peace and a vocal opponent of imperialism. Carnegie was gregarious and endlessly

1

energetic in all his pursuits, had a remarkable memory, and was an enrapturing conversationalist and storyteller. He was also at times unscrupulous in his dealings with others, vain, mendacious, hypocritical, and occasionally on the wrong side of the line between honest business dealings and those that would now be characterized as "conspiracies against the public."

When he retired from business affairs in 1901 after selling Carnegie Steel Corporation to J. P. Morgan for almost $500 million to form U.S. Steel, Carnegie's share of the sale proceeds consisted of 5 percent gold bonds worth approximately $226 million in 1901 dollars. The rest of his life, until his death in 1919, was spent giving that fortune away as well as acting as a vociferous advocate for world peace. The legacy of that last period in his life includes the Carnegie Corporation of New York, the Carnegie Endowment for International Peace, the Carnegie Foundation for the Advancement of Teaching (until recently the Teachers Insurance and Annuity Association–College Retirement Equities Fund, and now just TIAA), the Carnegie Institute, the Carnegie Institution of Washington, the Hero Funds, the Carnegie Institute of Pittsburgh (the precursor of what later became Carnegie-Mellon University), the Scottish Universities Trust, the United Kingdom Trust, more than 2,800 free public libraries, and a private pension list with an annual outlay of $250,000 that included former employees, friends, politicians, former U.S. president William Taft, the widows of presidents Theodore Roosevelt and Grover Cleveland, celebrities, and absolute strangers on whom he took pity.

This book follows Carnegie's rise to wealth and subsequent philanthropy through his actions as a business and economic entrepreneur. It also relates the ways in which he used or took advantage of political and governmental means to divert resources from other uses into those profitable for him and his partners. The order of presentation is roughly chronological. The first chapter presents the basic entrepreneurial context within which Carnegie's actions will be discussed. Following chapters move from his poverty-stricken childhood in Scotland to his youthful employment in the Pittsburgh, Pennsylvania, area; his rise within management in the Pennsylvania Railroad; his first investments and independent business ventures; the building of his manufacturing empire; and, finally, his major acts of philanthropy following the merger of that empire into U.S. Steel, the world's first billion-dollar corporation.

Andrew Carnegie was a major economic actor in the pre–World War I industrialization of America, and he has been both venerated and condemned by historians and biographers for his actions during that period. What is presented here as an economic biography is an attempt to use some of the tools of economics to better understand his actions and their effects, whether viewed as positive or negative. Most notable is the discussion of the Homestead lockout and strike of 1892, which illustrated a clash of visions of industrial relations and marked Carnegie for life in the public mind. My interpretation of that clash is neither exoneration nor censure. It is merely an attempt to shed new light on an old discussion. As always, it is up to the reader to decide whether I have succeeded.

Chapter One

Entrepreneurial, Entrepreneurship, and Entrepreneurs

The nouns *entrepreneur* and *entrepreneurship*, and the adjective *entrepreneurial*, are ubiquitous in the business and economic press of the twenty-first century. Awards are given for entrepreneurial activities or to the "Entrepreneur of the Year." An increasing number of colleges and universities have programs in entrepreneurial studies and centers for entrepreneurship. Nevertheless, what is meant by those words by those who use them is not always the same, and even sometimes ambiguous or otherwise unclear.

Entrepreneurship is typically used to characterize business activities that generate new ideas/products or that introduce novel production processes. These activities represent a break from the ordinary, a tectonic shift in the business world. Often, this *entrepreneurship* can easily be traced to the actions of particular men or women. And there is no doubt that some firms are more dynamic and creative in economic value than others. Of course, to say that a firm is entrepreneurial because there's an entrepreneur at its head is no explanation. It just takes us in a circle.

Yet the word *entrepreneur* is often used to refer to top managers, or to single owners of business firms, who are somehow more active than other managers or owners in pushing new products or new techniques to make existing products. *Entrepreneurship* is then used to indicate their primary function, while *entrepreneurial* describes their creative actions. There is a kernel of truth in doing this, but understanding why that is so requires a clear understanding of the "somehow." Otherwise, the labels fall to the level of the words *hero*, *heroic*, or *heroism*, each of which is often applied nowadays to almost anyone who does anything that is considered praiseworthy.

A similar approach to a definition is to attribute unique "creative" qualities to the entrepreneur, but this only raises the question of what those qualities are. As we'll soon see, one famous economist made just such an argument and tried to list the relevant qualities. Unfortunately, as we'll also see, he apparently spun the whole cloth of his argument out of thin air.

If entrepreneurship can be taught, then it is difficult to understand why all graduates of such programs are not equally successful in creating new ideas/ products/processes. One also might wonder why those teaching it are not themselves doing it, if they know what it is. An old critique of fortune tellers is that if they can peer into the future, they should be too busy getting rich to waste their time telling fortunes. Yet we do think entrepreneurship exists, and we usually associate it with the creation of new value, and we typically don't apply the term indiscriminately to business owners or top managers.

So, what exactly is this entrepreneurship, and what is the essence of entrepreneurial actions that distinguishes them from managerial or organizational ones? If we can understand that difference, it will be possible to understand which of Andrew Carnegie's actions were entrepreneurial and in what way such actions were formative of the growth and development of the economy of the nineteenth-century United States.

Attempts to provide a definition and explanation of entrepreneurial actions began with the eighteenth-century Parisian banker and economic theorist Richard Cantillon (1680s?–1734). Cantillon was an Irishman who made a fortune through speculation in Paris during the period of the "Mississippi Bubble." This took place in 1717–1720 and became perhaps the most famous monetary scandal in European history. One of Cantillon's business associates was John Law (1671–1729), a Scottish monetary theorist, who was appointed head of the central bank of France in 1716 by the country's regent, the Duke of Orleans. By the next year Law had become the controller-general of all French governmental financial affairs as well as founder and head of the Mississippi Company. This company was charged with developing the lands of the vast French-owned Louisiana territory in North America, as well as managing the trade between the colony and France.

John Law convinced the French government to finance its overall spending through the magic of printing and issuing paper money using the central bank he headed. As paper money flooded the country, people eagerly sought investments as the road to wealth and Mississippi Company shares skyrocketed in price, benefiting Law and anyone owning them. Cantillon was among those who bought shares while their prices rose, but he was one of the very few who sold what he had purchased when he decided that the whole scheme was about to collapse—as it subsequently did. Cantillon had become a multi-millionaire, while Law was bankrupted by his own scheme and forced to flee the country.

Cantillon's posthumously published *Essai sur la nature du commerce en general* (1755) presented the first systematic and general economic model with a central role for the entrepreneur. As Cantillon saw it, the profits of the entrepreneur in a market economy were earned as a result of his ability to conquer the uncertainty of the future through successful forecasting—as Cantillon had actually done in gaining his great wealth through speculation on the future share prices of the Mississippi Company.

Next on the historical stage in defining entrepreneurship was Adam Smith (1723–1790), moral philosopher and author of the most influential treatise on the theory of an economy of cooperating strangers that has ever been written. In *An Inquiry into the Nature and Causes of the Wealth of Nations* (1776), Smith argues that the profit rewards of the successful "undertaker"—that is, entrepreneur—are received because he "hazards his stock [of capital]," and his profits are in proportion to the size of that stock. While Cantillon had argued that the entrepreneurial essence is found in the ability to cope successfully with uncertainty, Smith argued that it consists of taking the risk of investing capital.

From those early beginnings until the present day, general agreement among economic and business theorists on the essence of entrepreneurship has not occurred. Nevertheless, three major theories have come to dominate its discussion.

The first is that of University of Chicago economist Frank Knight (1885–1972), author of *Risk, Uncertainty and Profit* (1921). Knight argued that risk could be quantified in the probability distribution of various possible outcomes of an investment activity. Knowing the probability of possible outcomes made them insurable, much as knowing the probability of rain helps one decide whether to carry an umbrella.

Rather than the risk associated with various possible outcomes, the main problem the entrepreneur/manager faces, according to Knight, is the unavoidable uncertainty of future events. If the future were completely foreseeable, there would be no "pure" profits. The competition between business firms to secure the resources to produce the goods desired by consumers would eliminate the difference between the prices of goods and all the costs of their production, one of which is a return for the productive services of capital. While the costs of resources would rise as competitors vied with one another to obtain them, the prices of the goods produced would fall as their supplies increased until "pure" profit was eliminated.

It is the uncertainty of the future due to the constantly changing circumstances of social life that makes possible a return to capital that is higher or lower than its "productive" reward share, argued Knight. It is that uncertainty that makes "pure" profit a residual, rather than a payment for services. The entrepreneurial opinions, foresight, and confidence of those who control the use of resources, rather than certain knowledge or insurable risk, guide judgments of how to use resources in the face of uncertainty. It is these judgments, together with good or bad luck, that are the source of "pure" profits or losses, and some men are better at judging than others. [1]

The second major theory of entrepreneurship was developed by New York University's Israel M. Kirzner (born 1930), a leading theorist of the Austrian School of Economics. Kirzner views his theory as an extension and further development of the theory of "functional entrepreneurship" of his teacher, Ludwig von Mises (1881–1973). In his magisterial economic treatise, *Human Action* (1949), Mises uses uncertainty as a springboard for his entrepreneurship theory, but with a decided difference from Knight. For Mises, all human action takes place in the face of an uncertain future and this gives all human action an entrepreneurial dimension. Rather than restricting the concept to business leaders or managers, Mises applies it to all economic actors, whether they are consumers, farmers, laborers, lenders, capitalists, or speculators.

More specifically, for Mises, it is the uncertainty of future prices (benefits) and costs (sacrifices) and the search for future profit (net gain) opportunities in the context of an exchange economy that constitute the entrepreneurial aspect of all decision making. This makes entrepreneurial action "the driving force of the market," and the function it performs is to tend to reduce future differences between prices (benefits) and costs (sacrifices)—however defined—for all economic actors. As in Knight's argument, it does so because actions taken to exploit a perceived future profit opportunity require resources to be bid away from less valued uses, tending to raise their costs to those who use them. The increased supply of the commodity that results from the use of those resources tends to reduce its price below what it would have been otherwise. Prices and costs thus tend to merge in the absence of further changes. Since market conditions are in constant flux through time, prices and costs may never actually meet. The former may be above or below the latter, depending on the accuracy of perceptions of profit opportunities and the actual actions taken in their pursuit. Because market conditions are constantly changing, uncertainty is always present in all decision making, giving it an intrinsic entrepreneurial dimension.

Israel Kirzner's concept of entrepreneurship begins with Mises's, and then refines and extends it. In an early work, *Market Theory and the Price System* (1963), Kirzner presents his market theoretical context for entrepreneurship. It is a vision of a market composed of individuals who act as demanders in some contexts and suppliers in others. They are purposeful participants in exchanges, with limited knowledge of market conditions. They are constantly making plans, taking actions to pursue them, and interacting with other participants such that plans and actions change when they can't be carried out exactly as intended. Everyone searches to buy at a lower price and sell at a higher one, but agreement on prices is neither always nor easily achievable. Thus, the plans and actions of every participant are a constraint on those of every other one. Nevertheless, as time passes, the tendency is for greater consistency in the plans and actions of all participants as they learn more about the plans and actions of others. Kirzner calls this scenario "the market process."

The uncertainty of the outcomes of plans and actions brings in the entrepreneurial element of speculation that identifies profit possibilities. Entrepreneurship is the perception and exploitation of such possibilities. The result benefits all participants as resources are moved from lower-valued uses to higher-valued ones, from lower- or no-profit uses to higher-profit ones. Later, in *An Essay on Capital* (1966), Kirzner argues that what is considered "capital" is completely dependent on the entrepreneurial appraisal of resource users who are following production plans based on speculations of profit possibilities. The function of capital goods is to shorten the production process by augmenting labor, and if plans change, or cannot be realized, what once were capital goods may suddenly become scrap.

A refinement in Kirzner's concept of entrepreneurship is introduced in *Competition and Entrepreneurship* (1973). He asserts that every participant in the market process possesses an aspect of consciousness that consists of being "alert" to profit possibilities. Later, in his *Perception, Opportunity and Profit* (1979), he argues that "alertness" makes possible a spontaneous movement from ignorance to knowledge of a profit possibility and it differs in quality from person to person. Actions to take advantage of such possibilities lead to increased knowledge of market conditions, which leads to better coordination among market participants. Nevertheless, it is the entrepreneurial alertness that spurs participants to action and to better knowledge of market conditions.

A further refinement occurs in Kirzner's *Discovery and the Capitalist Process* (1985). There, "alertness" becomes the "motivated propensity of man to formulate an image of the future" and to envision how to create it (Kirzner, 1985, p. 56). The motivation is still pure profit seeking, although competition stimulates it. Entrepreneurship itself is costless and unlimited in supply. In his early work, Kirzner argued that entrepreneurial action boils down to "arbitrage"—that is, it amounts to buying at lower prices and selling at higher ones. Later, he expanded his concept to include the innovation of new production processes and products, and the discovery of new resources.

The third major theory of entrepreneurship is an apparent historical artifact, although its author cites no historical sources or particular historical persons as origins of his theory. Joseph A. Schumpeter (1883–1950) was an Austrian émigré who first outlined his theory of the entrepreneur in his *Theory of Economic Development* (1911), which he revised in 1926 and was subsequently translated into English in 1934. Schumpeter envisions the entrepreneur as a unique and dynamic individual human being, who possesses both a strong will and an urge to be creative, unlike the dull mass of mankind. He is driven by the desire to gain social power by introducing and producing new products or new qualities of existing products. He uses new production processes, introduces new forms of organization, exploits new markets, or finds new sources of supply. He forces his products on a public initially resistant to anything new.

Schumpeter's entrepreneur saves or borrows the money needed for these innovations. He is no inventor himself, but in his role of innovator he uses whatever inventions happen to be lying about. The result of his actions is a burst of economic development from the inside of an economy, transforming it and raising it to a higher level of wealth and complexity. His competitors are either destroyed or forced to adopt the innovations of Schumpeter's entrepreneur in order to survive. As they do this, the temporary high profits of the original innovating entrepreneur are eroded away and the economy stabilizes at the higher level of development, only to await the next burst of innovation.

Later, in his *Capitalism, Socialism, and Democracy* (1942), Schumpeter argues that capitalism as a form of social organization is a "process of creative destruction" driven by an entrepreneurial elite, and that innovation will eventually become a routine aspect of giant corporations. When this is complete, an entrepreneurial elite will no longer be necessary and the economy will be transformed into a socialistic one—a victim of its own success.

The problem with Schumpeter's grand concept of the entrepreneur, this unique being who leads society to ever higher peaks of production and wealth, is that he fails to inform us of the source from which it sprung. It may be a product of Schumpeter's imagination, perhaps created by stereotyping historical persons or periods of industrial development, but who knows? Schumpeter's entrepreneur is a *deus ex machina*, an internal force of production apparently created *ex cathedra*—that is, on his authority. It is a stirring vision that unfortunately runs counter to the very foundational concept of modern economic analysis—the consumer as source of market demand and, consequently, driver of market supply.

From the latter part of the nineteenth century to the twenty-first, the basic assumption of non-Marxian development and growth theories of market economies is that both development and growth are driven by the demand side of the market. It is the anticipation of what commodities consumers will buy that spurs the investment to produce them. Entrepreneurship is inspired by perceived future market conditions. In Frank Knight's theory of entrepreneurship, as in that of Mises and Kirzner, consumers drive the market, and entrepreneurship arises out of the uncertainty of those future market conditions and the desire to anticipate them.

Schumpeter's entrepreneur resembles an "ideal type"—an explanatory device for historical studies that was first outlined by the sociologist Max Weber (1864–1920). According to Weber, an "ideal type" is an abstract representation of a historical figure or phenomenon that can be used as an explanatory device. It is obtained by comparing "scattered and discrete individual phenomena," and then identifying and intensifying common aspects to obtain an ideal conceptual representation or "type" (Mises, 1960, p. 76). Examples include representations of types of persons like "the warrior," or "the capitalist," or "the evangelist"; representations of periods of history like "the Middle Ages" or "the Reformation"; and representations of concerted activities like "mercantilism," or "imperialism," or "capitalism."

Schumpeter's conceptual entrepreneur appears to fit Weber's concept of an "ideal type," although he does not reference Weber (his contemporary). If it is an ideal type, then it is only useful as a device for historical typology. It allows us to type our historical players so they can be part of our attempt to show how they fit into the grand scheme of people and events that constitute history. But we can't use it to explain that history. We can't use it as a theoretical device to provide principles that explain why and how an individual person's actions met with success or failure. Individual actions determine particular outcomes, and only theory can tell us their importance and the reasons for their becoming.

For example, some prominent historical businessmen roughly fit the ideal type of Schumpeterian entrepreneur. They were innovators who disrupted industries and introduced new products and production processes. They were significant figures in business history. They are part of the story that history tells, and, although they were individuals, they possessed some important common characteristics. Why were they successful? Why did the products and production processes that they innovated disrupt existing markets and lead to industrial progress? Or did the innovations in question actually lead to progress instead of representing a malinvestment of resources that retarded economic growth and the production of wealth? That is what requires explanation. Market process theory tells us that they were successful if they anticipated consumer demand and, in so doing, introduced products and business practices that were superior to those of the past in the opinions of their customers and rivals.[2]

Andrew Carnegie was an entrepreneur in a Schumpeterian sense in that he was strong willed and wanted to gain social power, and he introduced new products and new processes and new forms of business organization. He channeled resources into the production of commodities and services that might not otherwise have been produced. That was his typology, his role in history. Why did he do these things successfully, and what did doing them mean for the economies of the late nineteenth century? Did those economies grow more or less rapidly as a result of his actions? Did his actions lead to more or less economic coordination?

To answer those questions, we need the theoretical concepts of the "entrepreneurial" aspects of human action and "the market process." We also need to examine the details of Carnegie's business and philanthropic ideas and activities. Ultimately, any individual person's actions are the result of the goals they pursue based on the values they choose in the context of what is possible. Those values are influenced by the ones dominant in that person's society, family, and associates, as well as by their own attempts at self-exploration and personal commitment to the attempt to thrive. Only with this knowledge in mind can we understand the actions, and the consequences of those actions, of Andrew Carnegie as an important actor in creating the history of the period under discussion.

In the pages that follow, I will primarily use the concept of Kirznerian entrepreneurship and entrepreneurial action for explanatory purposes, and I will place Andrew Carnegie firmly in the context of the market process. Because many of his actions and activities were directed at subverting that process, the result will be a fuller economic portrait of Carnegie and his role in nineteenth-century economic development than has previously been drawn.

Chapter Two

Early Life in Scotland

Andrew Carnegie was born on November 25, 1835, in a small stone cottage at the corner of Moodie Street and Priory Lane in Dunfermline, Scotland.[1]

As was the custom of the time, he was named after his paternal grandfather, a hand loom weaver from the nearby community of Pattiemuir. Andy's father, William, and his uncle, James, were also hand loom weavers, like their father and grandfather before them. They had moved from Pattiemuir to Dunfermline in 1830 to practice the art of weaving damask. Named after its origin in Damascus, this was fine linen cloth woven with elaborate patterns and designs. Dunfermline was its Scottish center of production.

Weavers in villages like Pattiemuir were independent craftsmen who marketed their own completed webs. At this point in the nineteenth century, that system was giving way to one of subcontracting with "manufacturers" in larger towns like Dunfermline. These middlemen would supply the pirns of thread, furnish common bleaching fields, and then dye and market the completed cloth, paying weavers by the piece (Wall, 1970, p. 32). It was this system of manufacture that Will and James Carnegie moved to join as subcontracting weavers.

Although manufacturers' investments in raw materials, warehouses, and inventories of cloth might have made them "the capitalists of the putting out system" (Murray, 1978, p. 15), the practice of paying the subcontracting weavers at a piece rate left the weavers especially vulnerable to downturns in the market for fine linen goods. Manufacturers could compensate through inventory management; weavers could not. This situation was compounded by the fact that "the most intricate fabrics were [the ones] most subject to sharp fluctuations in their levels of activity," as a result of seasonal variations in sales as well as in "the whims of fashion" (Murray, 1978, pp. 60–61). Consequently, damask weaving was more subject to the uncertainties of the future and thus more speculative than the weaving of plainer cloth, although it paid more in times of rising demand for luxury linens and their resultant higher prices.

The town of Dunfermline lies about fourteen miles north of Edinburgh across the Firth of the River Forth in the county of Fife. It had a population of only 11,500 when Andrew Carnegie was born, 5,044 of whom were engaged in weaving on 3,517 hand looms (Wall, 1970, p. 9). Small as it was in population, this virtually one-industry town had a thousand-year history that Carnegie learned as a boy. He would cherish and celebrate that history for the rest of his life. Ancient Dunfermline had been the capital city of a Scotland united under King Malcolm Canmore (d. 1093), defeater of the usurper Macbeth, in the mid-eleventh century. The town of Andy's youth still contained the ruins of Malcolm's royal palace and church. In fact, it was in the foundations of the ruins of the great abbey that had replaced the original church that the tomb of the fourteenth-century hero Robert the Bruce was discovered in 1818.

In 1835, this ancient town may have been the center of fine linen hand loom weaving in Scotland; yet it stood on the brink of the decline that would virtually eliminate that industry within two decades. Factories of power looms that had replaced the hand loom in cotton and woolen cloth production would soon do the same for the weaving of linen and silk.

After a few years of living and working in Dunfermline, Will Carnegie married Margaret "Mag" Morrison in December 1834. She was the daughter of a relatively prosperous shoemaker whose family lived just up the street, and whose radical political views matched Will's (Wall, 1970, p. 33). The newly married couple's rented cottage was both workplace and home, the ground floor serving as the weaving room while the cramped living quarters were in the attic room upstairs. It was there that Andy was born in a rustic bed built on the floor (Barr, 1947, p. 147).

Both the Carnegie and Morrison families were educated people and leading participants in the intellectual and political life of the town. Mag's father, Thomas Morrison, was the son of a wealthy Edinburgh leather merchant, and he married the daughter of another well-to-do merchant of that same town. Yet Thomas lost both his father's wealth and his wife's inheritance in a failed financial speculation.[2] The family subsequently moved to Dunfermline, where Thomas built up a successful trade as a shoemaker (Wall, 1970, p. 21).

Will Carnegie's father, nicknamed "Professor" or "Daft Andrew" by his peers, was an avid reader and participant in the "College of Pattiemuir," as the local circle of men interested in ideas and current events was called. Soon after Will and James moved to Dunfermline, "Daft Andrew" followed, and the political views he shared with the Morrisons led him and his sons to become active in similar circles. Thomas Morrison, his son Tom Jr. (or "Bailie"), his son-in-law George Lauder, and Will Carnegie were at the forefront of political agitation in Dunfermline.

The Carnegies and Morrisons were highly critical of the existing political and economic system in Scotland and England and became deeply embroiled in reform efforts in their writings, speeches, and other public acts. They were leaders in the political agitation that led to the adoption of the Reform Acts of 1832, and also in the Chartist movement that rose to importance in 1836.

The Reform Acts greatly broadened the male franchise by decreasing the property requirement; yet that requirement remained high enough that many, including the Carnegies and the Morrisons, were still excluded from the rolls of voters (Barr, 1947, p. 147). Chartists subsequently sought both political and economic equality and petitioned and demonstrated not only for complete elimination of the property requirement but also for universal adult male suffrage and parliamentary reform.

At a very early age, Andy sat next to his father as Will worked at the loom from dawn to dusk. As he grew older, other tasks were given him, and he might have become a weaver himself if the rapid decline of the hand loom industry had not led to his family's emigration to the United States in the summer of 1848. In this regard, luck favored young Andy. Rather than resembling some idealized picture of the independent weaver happily working away in the bosom of his family, working conditions of hand loom weavers were actually quite poor and worsening as years passed. Operating the loom itself required great strength, and the actions that actually wove the cloth involved repetitive and monotonous motions over long hours with both feet and hands.

The looms were worked in rooms that typically had dirt floors and were both poorly lit and unventilated. Consequently, the air in the room was oily and full of floating fibers, as well as a noxious gas emitted by the dressing materials used for the cloth. There were no indoor toilets, sanitation was poor, baths were largely unknown, and water was obtained from a communal well and brought into the house for cooking and limited washing. By the 1840s, the workweek was seventy to eighty hours, much of it taking place by candlelight. To top things off, like the rest of the population of the time, weavers and their families were subject to exposure to typhus, measles, whooping cough, diphtheria, smallpox, dysentery, diarrhea, and cholera (Murray, 1978, pp. 152–57).

Nonetheless, hand loom weavers were proud of their craft and "would always regard themselves in the same occupational class as goldsmiths, jewelers, and cabinet-makers" (Wall, 1970, p. 11). They looked down on coal miners and operators of power looms for cotton and wool. As a child, Andy Carnegie sat at the feet of such a skilled craftsman and aspired to be like him. As an adult, he would become a man who not only could quickly adapt to technological change but also would be in the forefront of those introducing it. His father became the other side of the coin—a man who could not, or would not, adapt—and he later died embittered and defeated in 1855 at the age of fifty-one.

Andy spent much of his free time as a boy with his uncle, George Lauder, and George's son, George Jr. (known as "Dod"). Uncle George was a history buff who owned a small grocery. In his spare time, he regaled both boys with the poems of Robert Burns and stories of Scottish history and its heroes: William Wallace, Robert the Bruce, and Sir John Graham. He also praised Washington, Jefferson, Franklin, and other founding fathers of the United States and railed against war and military display (Hendrick, 1932, vol. 1, p. 24).

In his autobiography, Carnegie notes how impressed he was as a child by the radical views of his relatives in favor of basic freedoms and in admiration of the American republic (Carnegie, 1920, p. 9). He also notes how proud his Uncle George's stories made him of his heritage, a pride that was later to prove of great benefit to Scotland—and Dunfermline in particular—as Carnegie's philanthropic plans formed and his income and wealth began to grow (Carnegie, 1920, pp. 15–16). His father, Will, and uncle-in-law, Andrew Aitkin, had contributed their books, along with those of other weavers, to what became the Tradesmans' and Mechanics' Library in 1831 (Thomson, 1903, p. 308). This was the beginning of what was to become the Carnegie Free Library fifty years later, only one of a wealthy Andrew Carnegie's many financial gifts to the town.

Andy also learned a great deal about the rewards of initiative during his childhood. One of his tasks when he was eight years old was to fetch water from the common well on Moodie Street. The custom was to line up buckets the night before, each bucket reserving a place in the line. Carnegie grew tired of seeing others arrive after him but take up their places in the line ahead. So, one morning he fetched his water soon after his arrival, jumping the line, and did the same from then on. He later claimed that he had early "developed the strain of argumentativeness, or perhaps combativeness," from arguing over places in that bucket line (Carnegie, 1920, p. 14). He had likewise learned that taking the initiative paid off. (It is also worth pointing out that "first come, first served" is a more time-efficient way of getting a commodity distributed than waiting for a queue to form before doing so. Andy's actions marginally contributed to that increased efficiency and may have stimulated others to do the same.)

Another example of his initiative is found in how young Andy solved the problem of feeding the offspring of two rabbits that his father had given him. His mother informed the boy that he could only keep them if he could find a way to feed them without raiding the family's garden. His solution was to trade the naming right for a baby rabbit to each one of his friends in return for a regular supply of the necessary clover and dandelions—an early act of subcontracting. As an adult, Andy would later remark that this was evidence of the "organizing power upon the development of which my material success in life has hung—a success not to be attributed to what I have known or done myself, but to the faculty of knowing and choosing others who did know better than myself" (Carnegie, 1920, p. 24).

Carnegie is too modest in his remarks. It may have been necessary for him to find others who knew where to gather sufficient clover and dandelions and to do the actual feeding, but it took an alert young Andy Carnegie to think of how to provide the incentive for them to do so. This is an early expression of the entrepreneurial element in his personality that would bear such great fruit years later.

Weavers in Dunfermline attained the highest incomes they would ever achieve during the years 1790–1812, which was the "Golden Age" of hand loom weaving (Murray, 1978, p. 8). Linen weaving dominated in the east of Scotland, as cotton weaving did in Glasgow in the west. The relatively high incomes of linen weavers attracted many more men into that craft. Further, someone with very little capital could set up as a "manufacturer" in the putting-out system, and then subcontract work to the independent weavers. Ease of entry made for fierce rivalry between Scottish manufacturers and provided a strong incentive for price competition in the marketing of finished cloth.

After 1826, manufacturers began to consign goods "to overseas agents upon advances given by these agents, instead of selling their goods directly to merchants" (Murray, 1978, p. 70). If the sale price was less than expected, manufacturers could cut their losses by paying weavers less. Both the rising supply of weavers and the falling prices of cloth served to drive down the incomes of weavers for thirty years following the "Golden Age." Also during that period, the production and exportation of linens in Germany and Russia grew continuously (Murray, 1978, p. 66). Consequently, all Scottish hand loom weavers' wages and living standards trended downward until, by the 1840s, "many weavers lived at a level little short of actual starvation" (Murray, 1978, p. 46).

When Andy was born in 1835, the hand loom weavers of Dunfermline were still relatively prosperous, although their average incomes had fallen from thirty pounds a year in the "Golden Age" to approximately twenty-two pounds in the mid-1830s (Murray, 1978, p. 90). Two years earlier, the United States had dropped all tariffs on the linen products that were the main products of the town. As a result, by 1836, "more than half of the fine linens produced in Dunfermline were being shipped to America" (Nasaw, 2006, p. 6). Will Carnegie was so encouraged that he moved his family to a larger cottage on Edgar Street, where he bought three more looms; he and three apprentices then worked the four looms in the downstairs room (Wall, 1970, p. 36).

This situation was not to last. There were now more than fifty manufacturers in the town, and the weavers struggled with them for higher rates by striking (Thomson, 1903, p. 329). Will Carnegie was on the strike committee when the Panic of 1837 in the United States struck a devastating blow to the trade in damask linens. The financial debacle decreased the income and wealth of upper-income American families, who were the best customers for fine linens, and this in turn reduced their purchases. Declining trade in fine linens meant declining prices and sales and production volume in Scotland. The unemployment rate in Dunfermline was 40 percent by September 1837 (Nasaw, 2006, p. 9). There were also outbreaks of typhus, influenza, and measles (Thomson, 1903, p. 331).

Nevertheless, by the next year trade was on the upswing again, and the weavers of Dunfermline were back at work. Two years after that, economic conditions again worsened, and the 1840s became a period of serious decline for the hand loom weaving of fine linens—one from which the industry would never recover.

Will Carnegie could find so little work that the family was forced to move back to another small cottage on Moodie Street, where Mag not only opened a small-scale grocery store in the work room but also began to sew shoes at night for her brother, Tom, after she closed the store. Andy's sister, Ann, was born in 1840, but she unfortunately died the next year during the recession and poor economic conditions of 1841. In the fall of that year there was a general strike, in the forefront of which stood Tom Morrison. Dragoons from Edinburgh were brought in to quell the mobs and clear the streets (Thomson, 1903, p. 335).

In 1842, U.S. tariffs were reestablished for linens, with predictably adverse results for the weavers of Dunfermline. From an average of eighteen shillings a week in 1836, weavers' incomes had fallen to ten to twelve shillings, barely enough to pay for a family's basic necessities (Thomson, 1903, p. 368; Murray, 1978, p. 108). By the next year, Will had sold all but one of his looms, and Mag's income became the dominant one for the family (Wall, 1970, p. 58). Andy's younger brother, and later business partner in many of his enterprises, Thomas, was born into the family's reduced circumstances of 1843.

Despite the Carnegie family's poor financial situation, Andy attended Robert "Snuffy" Martin's Rolland School on Priory Lane from the age of eight until shortly before emigrating to the United States in 1848. Martin used the Lancastrian, or factory school, method of rote memorization, in which he taught the older children and they taught their juniors what they had learned (Nasaw, 2006, p. 16). There, Andy learned basic literacy and arithmetic. He did well in school; apparently, he did so well that other students referred to him as "Snuffy Martin's Pet" (Wall, 1970, p. 46). It was also in Martin's school that Andy earned his first penny by successfully reciting a poem by Robert Burns that was Martin's favorite (Wall, 1970, p. 46). Carnegie was noted for his prodigious memory all his life, and it is not surprising that he would excel in a school that prized rote memorization. Under the influence of his Uncle George, he had memorized most of Burns's important poems even before he could read (Hendrick, 1932, vol. 1, p. 26).

When Andy was ten, he began to run errands and keep accounts for his mother's little grocery shop. He also threaded needles for her as she stitched shoes at night for her brother's business, and he sold gooseberries for his Uncle George (Hendrick, 1932, vol. 1, pp. 29, 38). It is wryly amusing that when his schoolmaster, Mr. Martin, called on him one day to quote a biblical proverb, Andy said, "Take care of your pence, the pound will take care of themselves" (Wall, 1970, p. 44).

That period of time at Martin's school was to be the only formal schooling Andrew Carnegie would have in his life, aside from classes in double-entry bookkeeping that he later took in Pittsburgh and other such skill-focused learning. As an adult, he was essentially self-taught in literature, history, politics, finance, management, and economics, and, like many self-taught individuals, he was fond of sprinkling his speeches and writings with quotations from Shakespeare and other literary classics in order to illustrate his learning.

In the summer of 1847, a steam-power weaving factory was established on Pitmuir Street that employed four hundred weavers making fine linen (Wall, 1970, p. 64). This was the death knell for the hand loom weavers of Dunfermline. Those who could not find employment in the factory now had only the coal mines to the east or the building of the railroad south of town as area alternatives. By that winter, Will Carnegie was no longer able to find any outlet for his skill in weaving and had ceased working (Nasaw, 2006, p. 22). He would never be employed at his trade full time after that and made few efforts to work at any other trade for the remaining years of his life.

Mag Carnegie's younger twin sisters, Anne and Kitty, had emigrated with their husbands, Andrew Aitkin and Thomas Hogan, to the United States in 1840, along with Mag's brother, William Morrison. The Aitkins and Hogans settled in Allegheny City, Pennsylvania, while Morrison chose East Liverpool, Ohio, about thirty miles northwest of them. Correspondence with Mag's sisters in the early 1840s had not been encouraging concerning employment conditions in America, but by the mid-1840s circumstances were very positive, and the Carnegies began to discuss leaving Scotland for the United States. The severity of the winter of 1847 convinced Mag that it was time to go (Wall, 1970, p. 68).

Their meager savings, the proceeds from the sale of Will's last loom and their few household goods, a loan of twenty pounds from Mag's friend Ailie Ferguson Henderson, and a gift of two pounds, ten shillings from Will's sister, Charlotte Drysdale, were all they had to make the trip. It was just enough. In July 1848, the Carnegies boarded the 380-ton former Maine whaling ship, the *Wiscasset*, in Glasgow's port on the Clyde, Broomielaw, and set sail for America (Nasaw, 2006, p. 25).

Chapter Three

Youth in Western Pennsylvania

Twelve-year-old Andrew Carnegie was short in stature with small, well-formed hands and feet. A square head with very light blond hair, blue eyes, a pinkish-ivory complexion, and a thin-lipped mouth sat on the narrow shoulders of his slight frame (Hendrick, 1932, vol. 1, p. 53). During the six weeks it took the *Wiscasset* to sail from Glasgow to New York City, young Andy quickly became a prized pupil and favorite of the crew. His intense curiosity concerning every detail of the ship and the sailing of it led him to roam constantly about the vessel asking questions. He also volunteered to run errands for crewmen, such as carrying messages to the other passengers. Within a year's time, this experience was to prove extremely valuable (Wall, 1970, pp. 73–74).

Nevertheless, as all good things do, the voyage and Andy's education at sea came to an end when the *Wiscasset* entered the New York harbor. Decades later, in his autobiography, Carnegie expressed the great regret he felt at having to leave the ship when it docked (Carnegie, 1920, p. 27). As just one of the happy endings he would arrange for himself after becoming wealthy, he eventually would have his own grand yacht, the *Seabreeze*, to sail the Atlantic seaboard and the coast of Scotland—and he would fund another, the *Carnegie*, with the task of remapping the oceans.

After a brief stay in New York, three more weeks of travel by coaches, canals, railcars, and steamers into the country's interior were necessary before the Carnegies finally arrived in Allegheny City to join Mag's sisters and their families. Annie Aitkin, recently widowed, now shared a house with her sister and brother-in-law, Kitty and Tom Hogan. It was one of two that stood on jointly owned property at 336 Rebecca Street (Nasaw, 2006, p. 30). The other was a cottage on the back of the lot where Tom Hogan's brother, Andrew, lived and operated a weaving trade. The Carnegie family moved into two upstairs rooms in the cottage and began to look for work.

At that time, Allegheny City had a population of about twenty thousand— only ten thousand less than Chicago—while across the Allegheny River to the south, at the junction of the Allegheny and Monongahela rivers, was Pittsburgh, a city of ninety thousand. Both cities were centers of heavy industry, which filled the air—and the lungs—of the population with ash, soot, and smoke, much of which settled on the surrounding land, buildings, and people, coating every exposed surface. Allegheny City was periodically flooded by the river, there were occasional fires in the town's mostly wooden buildings, and its unpaved streets became mud holes after every rain. Lacking a municipal water and sewage system, the resulting poor sanitation led to recurring cholera epidemics in the city (Nasaw, 2006, pp. 30–31). Such were the daily living conditions of the American refuge to which the Carnegies had fled from the unemployment and poverty of the declining hand loom weaving trade in Scotland.

At first, Will Carnegie tried to return to his craft of hand loom weaving. When Andrew Hogan decided to give up his own attempt to make a living by it, Will took over Hogan's weaving shop and leased his loom. Unfortunately, Will Carnegie had no more success in the business than had Hogan. Mag Carnegie resumed the binding of shoes for a local cobbler, Henry Phipps, for $4 a week (Wall, 1970, p. 81; Nasaw, 2006, p. 33).[1] Soon Will and Andy were both employed a mile away at the Anchor cotton textile mill, which was owned and operated by a Mr. Blackstock, a fellow Scot. In this, his first job since coming to America, Andy received the princely sum of $1.20 a week for working as a bobbin boy for twelve hours a day, six days a week.

Will Carnegie soon quit the mill and went back to his weaving, with no more success than before—a trade he was to continue until his death seven years later at the age of fifty-one. With her husband contributing little or nothing to the family income, Mag added Saturdays working with her widowed sister in Annie's grocery store. Meanwhile, Andy was hired away from the Anchor mill by John Hay, a bobbin manufacturer, for an increase in pay to $2 a week. His first duties were firing the boiler of the cellar steam engine and tending the running engine that ran the factory's machinery. Hay soon discovered that Andy could read and write and switched him to clerical duties, although the boy also had the job of dipping the newly manufactured bobbins in crude oil (Wall, 1970, p. 87). Andy's earlier recordkeeping for his mother's grocery in Dunfermline had prepared him for the clerical work, but the oil made him so nauseous that he afterward regarded that job as the worst he ever had (Carnegie, 1920, pp. 34–37).

Driven by ambition, and hoping to expand his accounting role in Hay's business, Andy and several of his friends spent evenings during the winter of 1848–1849 learning double-entry bookkeeping from a Pittsburgh accountant. Two of those friends—Thomas Miller and William Crowley—would later become key partners in Carnegie business enterprises. Yet Andy's accounting career plans were soon set aside in favor of an even better opportunity.

Uncle Tom Hogan knew David Brooks, the manager of the Pittsburgh telegraph office of the Atlantic and Ohio Telegraph Company. Brooks had employed one boy named George McLain to deliver messages to the various addressees in the city, but the business had grown so that now he needed a second messenger boy. Tom recommended Andy, who interviewed at the office at 100 Fourth Avenue, was hired, and was immediately put to work at $2.50 a week. Soon after, more messenger boys were needed, and Andy's friends Robert Pitcairn, David McCargo, and Henry W. Oliver were added to the office (Hendrick, 1932, vol. 1, pp. 55–58). All three would continue to be associated with Carnegie in his future business activities, as would Miller and Crowley. Carnegie was a man who made friends and, with few exceptions, kept them close all his life.

When Andy Carnegie and his friends became telegraph company messenger boys in 1849, it had been a mere seventeen years since Samuel F. B. Morse had conceived his version of the recording telegraph while on board a ship traveling from Le Havre to New York. Employed as professor of the literature of the arts of design at New York University, Morse completed the design of his telegraph, constructed a prototype, and filed his patent in 1837. A successful experiment with the new device at the Speedwell Iron Works in Morristown, New Jersey, took place three months later. Yet it was only by means of a grant of $30,000 obtained from Congress in 1843 that further experiments finally enabled Morse to send the famous message "What hath God wrought?" This occurred in 1844 over a line constructed on poles between Baltimore and Washington, D.C. Since then, under license either by the Morse patentees or by the rival patent of Royal E. House, telegraph lines had been strung between major cities on the eastern seaboard by numerous enterprising telegraph companies. While there were many independent companies steadily working their way westward across the continent, six of them united in an umbrella organization informally called the O'Rielly telegraph group (Reid, 1886, pp. 152–65).[2]

Under the Morse patent, Henry O'Rielly had organized the Atlantic Lake and Mississippi Valley Telegraph Company in 1845 to build a line from Philadelphia to Pittsburgh, with plans to later extend it west, north, and south to all major cities of the Midwest and the South. By December 29, 1846, the line was open for business to Pittsburgh, and David Brooks soon became the office manager. The O'Rielly firm reorganized in 1848, with the Philadelphia to Pittsburgh line as the Atlantic and Ohio Telegraph Company—one among the six nominally independent companies that composed the O'Rielly group (Reid, 1886, p. 165).

Andy's brief experience delivering messages from the crew of the *Wiscasset* to its passengers may have influenced Brooks's decision to hire him as a messenger boy for the telegraph company in 1849, but there can be no doubt about that decision's effect on young Carnegie's future. Within less than a year of landing virtually penniless in America, and possessing only a limited education, few skills, and an uncertain outlook, Andy Carnegie was in a position where his energy, ambition, diligence, and native intelligence would lead to a rapid rise in the business world. In little more than a decade he would become a highly paid manager for the Pennsylvania Railroad Company.

Eager to succeed in his new job in the telegraph office, Andy quickly began memorizing the street names and business addresses in the city. He also learned to recognize the telegraph company's customers by sight so that he could deliver their telegrams personally if he happened to see them on the street. More proof of young Carnegie's initiative is seen in the fact that, six months into the job, a suggestion from him solved a problem that frequently provoked quarrels among the other messenger boys. Telegrams delivered outside the downtown area required an extra charge of ten cents, which the delivering boy was allowed to keep. This sparked fierce competition to deliver those messages. Andy proposed that all the extra charges be pooled and divided equally among all messenger boys, which successfully ended the quarreling (Hendrick, 1932, vol. 1, p. 60). This would not be the last time that Andrew Carnegie would engage in "pooling" to abate rivalry among competitors. His own view of the incident was that this "cooperation" was his "first essay in financial organization" (Carnegie, 1920, p. 43).

Speaking of his early jobs as bobbin boy, steam engine tender, and messenger boy, Carnegie later said, "There was scarcely a minute in which I could not learn something or find out how much there was to learn and how little I knew" (Carnegie, 1920, p. 39). One of those areas in which he could now "learn something" was the result of his access to the day-to-day confidential communications of the Pittsburgh business and political community. He learned not only who was who but also much about their business and political relations. This ambitious young lad now knew by sight and had daily personal contact with the leading businessmen and politicians of his community (Wall, 1970, p. 92).

More immediately relevant to his own prospects for promotion was the fact that Andy could "learn something" in the telegraph office itself. He began to spend time in the operating room learning how to send and receive messages. Soon he was relieving the regular telegraph operators on breaks and assigned simple administrative tasks by office manager John P. Glass. He taught himself to take the messages by ear instead of waiting to transcribe the machine tape after the message had run. One result of these efforts was that Glass increased Andy's salary to $13.50 a month, a 20 percent premium over the $11.25 received by the other messenger boys. That raise caused him to tell his seven-year-old brother, Tom, that someday they would be rich and in business together as "Carnegie Brothers" (Wall, 1970, pp. 93–94). Decades later, this prediction came true.

Another result of Andy's growing competence was that he was sent to Greensburg, Pennsylvania, for two weeks in June 1851 as a substitute telegraph operator. He was now fifteen years old and making $4 a week, the same amount that his mother earned from binding shoes. This was to rise to $25 a month by the next year, when he was promoted to assistant operator, and he later became a full-time telegrapher at the age of sixteen (Carnegie, 1920, p. 59).

Less than four years after beginning work as a bobbin boy in a cotton mill, the monthly salary young Carnegie was earning had increased more than 500 percent as a result of his ambition, hard work, and willingness to take advantage of opportunities for advancement. His was now his family's main income. More important, his working conditions and the opportunity for further advancement had immeasurably improved. Prominent men in the business and political communities knew who he was and entrusted their most important messages to him (Wall, 1970, p. 102). He was also the operator who provided copies of incoming overseas press dispatches to all the local newspapers. The $1 a week that he was paid by them for doing this brought his total monthly income to $29, almost double his mother's earnings (Carnegie, 1920, p. 60).

It was at this point that an opportunity presented itself that was to set Andrew Carnegie firmly on the path that led to extraordinary wealth and international fame. By December 1852, Philadelphia and Pittsburgh were united by rail service by means of the almost-continuous single-track line of the Pennsylvania Railroad Company (PRR) (Burgess and Kennedy, 1949, p. 57). Like all railroads and canals originating on the eastern seaboard and extending westward into the interior of the country, the PRR was a solution to the problem presented by the mountain ranges that greatly impeded eastern access to western producers. Shipping by means of the Ohio, Missouri, and Mississippi rivers south to the port of New Orleans, or by way of the Great Lakes and Erie Canal to the port of New York, was circuitous, slow, and hazardous. Canals, like the Erie in New York or the Pennsylvania Main Line Public Works, required many locks to manage changes in elevation, making transportation necessarily slow. In addition, canals and lakes froze in winter, steamboat boilers occasionally blew up, and ships sank (Stover, 1997, p. 9).

Incorporated April 14, 1846, the PRR in 1852 consisted of three separate but linked rail lines. The first was its own constructed 249-mile single-track line from Pittsburgh to Harrisburg. The second was the leased single-track line of the privately owned Harrisburg, Portsmouth, Mt. Joy, and Lancaster Railroad from Harrisburg to Columbia, just west of Lancaster. The third was the state-owned eighty-one-mile double-track line of the Philadelphia and Columbia Railroad from Columbia to Philadelphia—which the PRR would purchase in 1857.[3] The only break in these linked lines was the thirty-six miles of the state-owned Allegheny Portage Railroad. This was a span of eleven levels and ten inclined plane tracks used to haul cars over the mountains between Hollidaysburg, just south of Altoona, and Johnstown, which was halfway between Altoona and Pittsburgh. This arrangement divided the PRR into eastern and western divisions.

The new superintendent of the western division of the Pennsylvania Railroad was twenty-eight-year-old Thomas A. Scott, a man later described as "the quintessential railroad man of his generation" by railroad historian Richard White (White, 2011, p. 3).[4] Scott decided that in order to more carefully dispatch and monitor rail traffic, he needed his own telegraph operator. Being one of the men who entrusted their most important messages to Andy Carnegie, Scott did not hesitate to offer the position to him. On February 1, 1853, at the age of seventeen, Andrew Carnegie became Scott's personal telegraph operator and private secretary, earning an initial salary of $35 a month.

Carnegie quickly settled into the job, sharing an office with Scott and using his position as Scott's secretary to increase his learning by absorbing all the information he could about the PRR and railroading in general. With the PRR position, his working conditions were greatly improved, his salary was higher, and his workday was shorter by four or five hours (Nasaw, 2006, p. 57). He soon convinced his friends David McCargo and Robert Pitcairn to quit their jobs as messenger boys and work for the PRR because of its better prospects for the future, as compared to those of the telegraph industry.

Despite this good beginning, Carnegie's career was almost nipped in the bud by an incident that occurred during his monthly trip to Altoona to pick up the payroll for Pittsburgh employees. Andy inadvertently dropped the payroll off the moving train while on a bridge over a mountain stream. Only by a fluke was he able to recover it, for luckily it hadn't fallen into the water (Carnegie, 1920, pp. 67–68). One can only imagine the consequences if it had so fallen and been swept away by the current.

While in Altoona he met Scott's boss, Herman Lombaert, who was the PRR's general superintendent at the time. Lombaert took the young man home to tea, introducing him as "Mr. Scott's 'Andy,'" to Carnegie's delight (Carnegie, 1920, p. 67). Five years later, when Lombaert became vice president of the railroad, Scott would be promoted to the position of general superintendent and both he and his protégé, Andrew Carnegie, would move to Altoona.

Carnegie's employment with the PRR began during a crucial period in that railroad's development. The former chief engineer who had directed the construction between Pittsburgh and Harrisburg—John Edgar Thomson—had just become PRR president in 1852. He would preside over its period of greatest expansion from that year until his death in 1874. Thomson was ambitious and tireless in the extension of the railroad's lines, in making constant improvements, and in arranging the financing to support both. He faced many serious obstacles to realizing that ambition, all of which he overcame in his twenty-two years as PRR president.

The state-owned Allegheny Portage Railroad was a major weakness of the rail connections between Philadelphia and Pittsburgh. Not only was it time-consuming to use stationary engines winding wire cables to haul the cars up and down inclined planes on the slopes to surmount the mountain barrier of the Alleghenies, but that route was also closed by ice and snow for three to four months in winter and by floods in the spring (Schotter, 1927, p. 4). In addition, the state refused to operate the portage railroad at night (Burgess and Kennedy, 1949, p. 55). The PRR's own double-track line over the Alleghenies, including a 3,570-foot-long tunnel, would not be completed until February 1854.

The PRR rails were made of wrought iron, and breakages and derailments were frequent. Its engines burned wood or coal, and train speeds were slow.[5] Nevertheless, passage by trains between Philadelphia and Pittsburgh took only thirteen hours instead of the four days it took on the Pennsylvania Main Line of Public Works' combination of canals, portage railroad, and the Philadelphia and Columbia Railroad. Railroad bridges were wooden and were frequently washed out, burned, or damaged by severe weather. Train collisions were not infrequent on the single-track lines from Columbia to Hollidaysburg and Johnstown to Pittsburgh. Also, telegraph lines broke, or were vandalized, interrupting communications between stations and managers and greatly complicating rail traffic.

Nonetheless, Andy Carnegie was at the right place at the right time. He was employed by the railroad that was to become "the gold standard of railroad lines, and the one that kept the best records" (White, 2011, p. 153). He was now personal assistant to the third assistant superintendent for the PRR, the one to whom all agents reported as an alternate to the general superintendent (Burgess and Kennedy, 1949, p. 86). After his promotion to general superintendent in 1858, Tom Scott would become a PRR vice president in 1860, then senior vice president, and finally the railroad's president following the death of J. Edgar Thomson in 1874. In his career, Scott would be manager, investor, speculator, and entrepreneur, like the other big names in this era of railroad building. Carnegie would learn by association. In addition, Carnegie was privy to all the equipment and infrastructure challenges faced by railroads, and he was enterprising enough to see the opportunities for improvement and self-enrichment. His association with Scott during the coming years would prove to be of great personal and financial advantage to him, as we shall see.

Chapter Four

On the Road to Wealth

The ambition and initiative that distinguished young Andrew Carnegie when he worked for the Atlantic and Ohio Telegraph Company continued to show itself in his new job with the Pennsylvania Railroad. As telegraph operator, secretary, and personal assistant to superintendent Thomas Scott, Andy was subordinate to Scott's authority, but he was also in a position to exercise that authority by proxy. An early example of this situation involved train orders.

Orders directing train movements and responding to accidents were often telegraphed, and only Scott had the authority to issue them. Unfortunately, when timely orders were needed, he was frequently out of the office dealing with wrecks and other problems on the single line between Pittsburgh and Johnstown. On one of those mornings a new accident was reported, and, rather than waiting for Scott's return, Andy telegraphed the necessary orders in Scott's name to resolve the problem. When Scott learned of this, he not only did nothing about it but also permitted Andy to continue doing so in the future. Carnegie later learned that the incident had come to the attention of J. Edgar Thomson himself, and favorably so. Of this youthful boldness Carnegie said, "The great aim of every boy should be to do something beyond his sphere of duties—something which attracts the attention of those over him" (Carnegie, 1920, p. 73).

Attract attention he had, and that was just his first step "beyond his sphere of duties." As he learned more of the daily operations of the railroad, his employer began to trust him with even greater authority. Scott occasionally left their offices in the twenty-acre Outer Depot to travel on business or for pleasure. Before one such trip, he appointed his young assistant acting head of the division. During Scott's absence, an accident occurred on a ballast train as a result of the negligence of several employees. Carnegie issued the orders needed to clear the wreck, suspended two of the men, and fired a third. On his return, Scott rejected appeals and let his subordinate's decisions stand (Wall, 1970, pp. 122–23). Years later, in reassessing what he had done, Carnegie admitted that he had been youthfully injudicious—even harsh—in his judgments at the time. He said, "Only experience teaches the supreme force of gentleness [for] light but certain punishment, when necessary, is most effective" (Carnegie, 1920, p. 74).

Attracting the attention of his superiors through his actions was not young Carnegie's only means of doing so. After its publication, he admitted to Scott that an unsigned letter to the *Pittsburgh Journal* defending the PRR against local criticism was his. As a result, he was invited to spend a Sunday in Greensburg, Pennsylvania, at the home of the PRR's chief counsel, Colonel Niles A. Stokes. Stokes apparently realized that Scott's young assistant was more than an ambitious and dedicated workman and deserved cultivation. "The pen was getting to be a weapon with me," commented Carnegie about this incident in his autobiography (Carnegie, 1920, p. 82). During his visit, he so admired an inscription on the mantel in Stokes's library that years later he would put it on his own library mantel in New York as well as on the one in his Scottish mansion, "Skibo":

> He that cannot reason is a fool.
> He that will not a bigot.
> He that dare not a slave. (Carnegie, 1920, p. 82)

After five years as assistant superintendent for the Western Division, Thomas Scott was promoted to general superintendent in January 1858, and he and Andrew Carnegie moved from Pittsburgh to Altoona, which was now the location of the PRR's main repair and construction shops. Andy's salary was increased to $50 a month.

Soon after their arrival, they became aware that workers in the shops were talking about a possible strike. According to Carnegie, one of the workmen gave him the names of the strike leaders because of a past good turn Andy had done him. Andy gave the list to Scott, who promptly fired everyone on it. The lesson learned for Carnegie was "[s]light attentions or a kind word to the humble often bring back reward as great as it is unlooked for" (Carnegie, 1920, p. 86). If the story is true, it is difficult to avoid the suspicion that the motive of the informant may have been something other than just returning a favor. There would have been considerable personal risk involved in informing against potential strike leaders to the general superintendent's young assistant. Carnegie was to use informants often in the future, especially to acquire useful information against business rivals. This may have been an early example of that practice.

One story that Carnegie relates of his period in Altoona that is certainly not true is his tale of how the Woodruff Sleeping Car came to the attention of Scott and the other officers of the PRR. According to Carnegie, a chance encounter with T. T. Woodruff on a train led to Woodruff showing him a model of his sleeping car. On his return to Altoona, Andy informed Scott of Woodruff's invention and arranged a meeting between the two men. The meeting led to a contract for the PRR to purchase sleeping cars from Woodruff, who then offered Carnegie a one-eighth interest in his company. Carnegie was able to finance it by borrowing the first monthly payment of $217.50 from a local bank and paying the rest from the dividends his one-eighth interest subsequently earned each month (Carnegie, 1920, p. 87).

As both Wall (1970, pp. 138–43) and Nasaw (2006, pp. 61–63) point out, Carnegie's story is pure fabrication. Documentary evidence tells a completely different story. Woodruff was a master car builder for the Terre Haute and Alton Railroad in Alton, Illinois. He had patented his sleeping car design in 1856; the first one was constructed in 1857. He approached the PRR in 1858 after several of his cars were already running on other railroad lines, including the New York Central. Carnegie's actual role was to serve as a "bagman" (Nasaw's term) for J. Edgar Thomson and Tom Scott, who made the contract with Woodruff on the condition that they received partial ownership in his company, that ownership to be held in Carnegie's name. Whatever the details of the arrangement between the three PRR men may have been, within two years Carnegie was receiving an income of $5,000 a year from his ownership shares in Woodruff's sleeping car company (Wall, 1970, p. 143).

This was not the first investment that Scott had steered Andy's way. Since March 1855, the PRR had contracted to carry Adams Express Company packages between Philadelphia and Pittsburgh (Nasaw, 2006, p. 59). While they were still in Pittsburgh in the spring of 1856, Scott offered his young assistant an opportunity to purchase ten shares of Adams Express stock from a Mrs. Ann Patrick for $600. She had previously bought them from the widow of the original owner, William Reynolds, but now needed to sell them. In his autobiography, Carnegie claimed the amount was $500 and that he got the money from his mother, who used their house as collateral to borrow it (Carnegie, 1920, p. 80). The truth of the matter, again as revealed by documentary evidence, was that Scott loaned Carnegie the $600 in return for a May 17, 1856, IOU for $610, payable within six months. By November 1, Carnegie had been able to save $200, and, using the Adams Express shares as collateral, he borrowed the rest from a "George Smith" at 8 percent to redeem the IOU. A year later, he made one payment to Smith of $100, and his mother mortgaged their home to get the remaining $300 to pay off the Smith note (Wall, 1970, pp. 133–34).

Meanwhile, Andy had received his first dividend of $10 in June 1856 from his Adams Express shares. His reaction to this "first penny of revenue from capital—something that I had not worked for with the sweat of my brow" was to shout, "Eureka! Here's the goose that lays the golden eggs" (Carnegie, 1920, p. 80).

The lesson he learned from these experiences was clear: income from shrewd investments trumped working for others. The trick was to identify the investments that paid. Today, what he, Scott, and Thomson did would be called "insider trading." They used their inside knowledge of the business relations of their employer with other companies for personal gain. Given that they were investing in firms that had contractual relations with the PRR that benefited those outside firms, they also might have been acting against their fiduciary responsibility to the PRR. If the Adams Express and Woodruff contracts with the PRR overly benefited those two companies because of the influence of these executives within the PRR, that would certainly be the case.[1] In any event, the lesson Carnegie took from these experiences was that he could use his insider's knowledge to his own profit, and he did so on many occasions in the future.[2]

In the fall of 1859, Tom Scott was promoted to vice president of the PRR and used his influence with Thomson to secure Andrew Carnegie's promotion to superintendent of the western division as of December 1. After little more than six and a half years working as Scott's assistant, Carnegie was going back to Pittsburgh at age twenty-four to head the office in which he had been first employed as a telegraph operator at $35 a month. His PRR salary was now $1,500 a year, while his current income from investments was several times that. He would take his sixteen-year-old brother, Tom, with him as his personal secretary and begin to groom himself in manners and dress and broaden his knowledge of literature and languages. He aimed to rise in society as he rose in wealth and knew that his few years of formal education as a boy in Dunfermline were no adequate preparation.

Andrew Carnegie had learned a lot during his years of working for Thomas Scott. When he and Scott moved to Altoona, the PRR's transportation superintendent was Herman Haupt. Haupt introduced a managerial system that required "detailed reporting and accounting from employees at all levels, as well as careful division of managerial responsibilities into so-called line and staff functions" similar to the military (Misa, 1995, p. 22). In addition to Haupt's lessons in managing a large enterprise and Scott's lessons in shrewd personal investment strategies, Andy also learned from Scott the importance of detailed cost accounting for operational decision making (Nasaw, 2006, p. 65). The accounting system of the PRR would become a model for him because it

> allowed much more refined measures of fiscal health than simple profit and loss. It forced distinctions between construction costs and operating costs and how expenses were to be allocated to each account. . . . It classified operating expenses in a way that allowed distinctions between fixed expenses and operating expenses with the "operating ratio" measuring the percentage of gross revenue . . . needed to meet operating costs. It made cost per ton-mile the major measure of railroad efficiency. (White, 2011, p. 375)

The principle implanted in young Carnegie's business philosophy was that cost reduction enabled price reduction as a competitive tool (Wall, 1970, pp. 171–72). Andy had also observed and learned that regular equipment and facilities repair, maintenance, and replacement activities were important means of maintaining (and preferably increasing) sales revenue. Lastly, and of most importance, he had learned the necessity of innovative capital investment and constant upgrades of facilities, equipment, and infrastructure (Nasaw, 2006, pp. 64–65).[3] All of this early knowledge would be consistently applied in his later entrepreneurial activities.

He also may have learned other useful practices. Just before the outbreak of war, Tom Scott "supervised the systematic bribery of the Pennsylvania legislature and manipulation of the press to remove the tax on freight passing over the Pennsylvania Railroad and substitute an annual payment" (White, 2011, p. 5). Scott had also arranged for the government to pay the PRR a standard rate for freight haulage, whether it was local or long distance.[4] This was a boon to the railroad because the average cost of transport fell with distance and Scott was able to secure rates that charged all shipments as if they were local (White, 2011, p. 6). Richard White's general assessment of Tom Scott is that "corruption became part of his very makeup." Of course, we have no way of knowing the degree to which young Andy Carnegie was aware of all this. He certainly doesn't mention such activities in his generally praiseful portrait of Scott in his autobiography and other writings. He also continued to partner with Scott in business ventures almost to the time of the latter's death in 1881 (Nasaw, 2006, p. 155).

Despite his now-elevated position in management, Andy's job after the return to Pittsburgh would be no picnic. Railroad life was rough then, and Carnegie worked hard and drove his men hard. He spent a lot of time in the open because wrecks were common. Because he was "riding by choice in the locomotive cab, sleeping frequently on the floors of freight cars, making himself at home in construction camps—the life certainly toughened the body, even if, at the same time, it had a tendency to harden the spirit" (Hendrick, 1932, vol. 1, p. 88). But Carnegie was up to the challenge; his qualities of "quickness of decision, assertiveness, absolute confidence in himself, and a willingness to accept responsibility" could now be fully exploited in his position as superintendent of the western division (Hendrick, 1932, vol. 1, p. 89).

After briefly residing in Pittsburgh, the Carnegies bought a house in the suburb of Homewood and now mixed socially with the prominent area businessmen and political figures who were their neighbors. Andy hired relatives, such as his brother, Tom, and cousin, Maria Hogan, as well as friends from his boyhood days, like David McCargo, to fill positions at the PRR.[5] He also continued his efforts at self-improvement under the tutelage of educated neighbors, people such as Leila Addison, whose mother had been tutored by Scottish essayist and historian Thomas Carlyle. Andy also became active in Republican Party circles. The pending Civil War would soon send him to Washington, D.C., as the transportation of troops, munitions, and supplies by railroad became crucial to both the Union and the Confederacy.

Simon Cameron, a former member of the board of directors of the Harrisburg, Portsmouth, Mt. Joy, and Lancaster Railroad, as well as the board of the PRR-controlled Northern Central Railroad, was now Abraham Lincoln's secretary of war. When Fort Sumter fell, Cameron called his friend Tom Scott to Washington, D.C., to be his assistant. Scott arrived there in April 1861, and Carnegie and a group of railroad workers and telegraph operators followed later, summoned by Scott to keep the tracks repaired and open, the trains running, and telegraph service maintained into and out of the city (Wall, 1970, pp. 160–68). Carnegie also supervised the laying of track and the erection of new telegraph lines, the rebuilding of the Long Bridge across the Potomac, and the stringing of telegraph lines in northern Virginia.

Once those tasks were completed, and after he had supervised the crucial rail and telegraph support for the Union Army at the Battle of Bull Run, Carnegie requested, and was granted, permission to return to his regular duties with the PRR. He arrived in Pittsburgh in September, resumed his superintendent duties, and continued to pursue his personal investment plans for the duration of the war. At this point Carnegie owned stock in several express, horsecar, and coal companies, as well as an oil company, an iron manufacturer, and Woodruff's sleeping car company (Nasaw, 2006, p. 75).[6] The only break in his management and investment activities from this time until the end of the war in 1865 was a triumphant vacation return to Scotland in the summer of 1862. When his name came up in the military draft in 1864, he bought a replacement (Nasaw, 2006, p. 84).

An early investment opportunity during the war years was offered to him by his Homewood neighbor, William Coleman.[7] While Carnegie had been in Washington in 1861, Coleman had formed the Columbia Oil Company to drill wells and produce oil in Titusville, Pennsylvania. The first productive well in Titusville had been drilled near Oil Creek in late August 1859 by "Colonel" Edwin L. Drake, and the oil rush was on. Coleman had purchased a five-hundred-acre farm in Titusville in 1859, and in 1861 he offered to sell Carnegie an interest in the company that would drill and extract the oil on the property. After an inspection trip to the area in late fall with Coleman, Carnegie bought more than one thousand shares in the company. His initial investment of little more than $11,000 returned $17,868.67 in dividends in only the first year of production (Wall, 1970, p. 176).

Another of his investments had actually been initiated in early 1861 when he and his boyhood friend, Tom Miller, formed the Freedom Iron Company to manufacture iron for railroad rails. At that time, Miller was employed as a purchasing agent for the Pittsburgh, Fort Wayne & Chicago Railroad. Later that year Miller invested in a small business owned by two brothers, Andrew and Anthony Kloman, who made and supplied railroad axles to his employer.[8] Following the insiders' practice of the day, his one-third interest in the Kloman brothers' firm was held in the name of his and Carnegie's mutual acquaintance Henry Phipps Jr., a bookkeeper for the firm of Dilworth & Bidwell.[9] The war made Kloman & Company prosperous and in need of expansion, which Miller also helped to finance. Dissension within the firm in 1863 between Anthony and Andrew Kloman led to Miller enlisting the help of his Freedom Iron partner, Andrew Carnegie, as arbitrator. The arbitration led to a recapitalization of the firm as Kloman and Phipps and the departure of Anthony Kloman.

As part of the deal, Carnegie brought his brother Tom into the Kloman and Phipps partnership. Kloman, Phipps, and Tom Carnegie subsequently forced Miller's departure. In retaliation, a new firm—the Cyclops Iron Company—was formed in 1864 by Miller and Carnegie in competition with Kloman. The result of all the moves and countermoves in this infighting mini-saga was the merger of the two firms in 1865 as the Union Iron Mills, with Andrew Carnegie as president and his brother Tom as vice president. Bad feelings continued between Miller and Phipps until finally Miller was bought out by Carnegie in 1868 and the firm renamed Carnegie, Kloman & Company. Carnegie now held, and would continue to hold, the controlling interest in this firm and its successors until the merger that would create U.S. Steel (Wall, 1970, pp. 239–55; Nasaw, 2006, pp. 85–88).

As if these business ventures of the early 1860s were not enough, in 1862 Carnegie decided that because iron bridges would soon replace wooden ones, it was time to get into the bridge-building business. He and three engineers, John Piper, Aaron Shiffler, and silent partner Jacob Linville—the chief bridge engineer for the PRR—formed Piper & Shiffler, a railroad bridge-building company that would soon be constructing bridges for the PRR and its various subsidiary railroads.[10] Two other silent partners were Tom Scott and J. Edgar Thomson (Nasaw, 2006, p. 80). In 1865, the company was reorganized as the Keystone Bridge Company to specialize in building cast-iron railroad bridges.[11] Later, the firm began to use wrought iron for the upper cord because it would bend if struck, not break, as would cast iron.[12] This important improvement would later result in getting them the January 1868 contract for the superstructure of a bridge across the Mississippi at Dubuque, Iowa (Carnegie, 1920, pp. 116–17).

Carnegie made many other investments during the war years. At the age of twenty-eight in December 1863, when he summed up his income for that year, it came to a total of $47,860.67, of which only $2,400 was his salary as third assistant superintendent for the PRR (Hendrick, 1932, vol. 1, p. 120).[13] By 1866, his major investments would include Columbia Oil, the Central Transportation Company (formerly the Woodruff Sleeping Car Company), Adams Express, and several banks and insurance companies. His main enterprises at that time included the Union Iron Mills, the Freedom Iron and Steel

Company, the Keystone Bridge Company, the Superior Rail Mill, and the Pennsylvania Locomotive Works (Hendrick, 1932, vol. 1, p. 137).

In early 1865, it was clear that the Civil War was coming to an end, with the Northern armies triumphant. Carnegie was busy engineering the merger that would become the Union Iron Mills and expanding the Keystone Bridge Company. Having concluded that investment and enterprise provided a far more lucrative and challenging field for his talents than railroad management, he resigned from the PRR in April 1865. Although his managerial career with the PRR came to an end, his investment and enterprise connections with the railroad, as well as partnerships with Tom Scott and J. Edgar Thomson, would continue for many years—and greatly to his financial benefit, as well as that of his partners.

It was time for a break. Andy, Henry Phipps Jr., and another friend, John Vandevort, left for an extended European tour in May. Nonetheless, Carnegie's business interests were never out of his mind. He regularly received reports from his brother, Tom, on their business interests during his travels, and he made side trips to visit iron mills in several countries (Nasaw, 2006, pp. 95–96). While Phipps and Vandevort toured Switzerland, Andy stayed in London and Paris working on a deal with people in London for the American rights to the Thomas Dodd process for facing iron rails with steel (Wall, 1970, pp. 233–34). Although iron rails lacked durability, steel rails were still far too expensive to be used extensively, and facing iron with steel seemed to be a promising lower-cost alternative.[14] The Union Iron Mills were to use the Dodd process, although continued strife among the Union Mills partners after Carnegie and Phipps's return in the spring of 1866 led to the departure of Tom Miller and the reorganization that resulted in Carnegie, Kloman & Company.

Unfortunately, Carnegie found that the Dodd process was faulty: it produced inferior rails that failed to sell despite his determined efforts to market them. Even Thomson at the PRR turned them down. So he next negotiated for the British Webb process to accomplish the same result. It, too, produced inferior rails and had to be abandoned (Wall, 1970, p. 258). Despite these failures, one thing is clear: Andrew Carnegie was alert to the needs of the future and saw innovation as a key competitive means for increasing the market for his product, something he would continue to pursue throughout his career. In fact, after the Freedom Iron Company was reorganized in 1866 as the Freedom Iron and Steel Company, Carnegie began the conversion to the Bessemer method of steel production as part of his attempt to make the

Webb process work. Although it didn't, and Freedom continued to produce iron rails, by 1868 it also could produce a limited amount of steel rails (Wall, 1970, pp. 259–60).

Carnegie, Kloman & Company (the former Union Iron Mills) supplied the iron parts for the Keystone Bridge Company, which received considerable business building bridges for the PRR. As president of the PRR and an investor in Keystone Bridge, J. Edgar Thomson was being paid to run the PRR in addition to receiving dividends from his Keystone Bridge shares for the business he was directing its way. In 1868, he increased his investment in the bridge company and also ordered the replacement of all PRR wooden bridges with iron ones (Nasaw, 2006, p. 103).

At the same time that one recognizes Thomson's self-serving actions and Carnegie's dependence on contracts with his former employer, one also must recognize that these two Carnegie enterprises were manufacturing and installing high-quality products using the latest technology. This is evidenced by the fact that his associated companies early attracted the attention of the Roebling brothers, the future builders of the Brooklyn Bridge—for which Carnegie's companies would later supply the structural beams, braces, and plates (Wall, 1970, p. 654). Carnegie's and Thomson's codependence, unethical though it seems to present-day observers, nonetheless mutually benefited their respective business concerns at the same time that it filled their pockets.

Whether other iron works and bridge companies could have better served the PRR is unknown. The success of Keystone Bridge in securing contracts from other railroads and government bodies in the face of competition suggests otherwise. Carnegie was especially successful in securing contracts for the building of bridges across the Ohio, Monongahela, Mississippi, and Missouri rivers. It was also his Keystone Bridge Company that secured the contract to build the superstructure of the massive Eads Bridge at St. Louis, the central span of which was required by congressional legislation to be an unprecedented minimum of five hundred feet.

Yet even here the PRR had a role to play because the railroad stood to benefit greatly from the bridge's existence. It would gain a terminal in St. Louis for its St. Louis, Vandalia, and Terre Haute line across southern Illinois that then terminated at East St. Louis on the Illinois side of the river.[15] It was also the case that the Illinois and St. Louis Bridge Company needed the influence and traffic of the PRR for its financial viability, and, with Tom Scott as a member of its board of directors, it had that influence. Needless to say, there would be benefits for any companies involved in the bridge's construction and in which PRR officers had investments—namely, Carnegie's two companies.[16] Given Scott's investment in the Keystone Bridge Company, it is not surprising that the superstructure contract for the bridge was awarded to Keystone.

Using his position as a powerful member of the board of directors of the Illinois and St. Louis Bridge Company, Tom Scott managed to get J. H. Linville, chief bridge engineer for the PRR, appointed as chief consultant on the bridge's design, although conflict between Linville and James Eads made that chief consultancy a brief one.[17] Of course, like Scott, Linville was also a silent partner in the Keystone Bridge Company, and his involvement in the bridge project necessarily continued.

There were considerable problems in manufacturing the parts of the superstructure caused by Eads's ever-changing designs and his demand that a high proportion of the components be steel rather than iron. As a result, the cost of the bridge continued to grow beyond projections and the expected completion date continued to recede into the future. Notwithstanding these problems created by Eads, Carnegie's companies and subcontractors combined innovative methods with rigorous quality standards and met Eads's requirements. This occurred in spite of Carnegie's initial and continuing skepticism concerning Eads's knowledge of bridge construction and his general competence (Jackson, 2001, pp. 104–7). After several weeks of Keystone holding the almost-completed bridge hostage for payment of fees and bonuses, the first foot traffic over the bridge finally took place on May 23, 1874 (Wall, 1970, p. 277).

In addition to his construction contract, Carnegie was involved in marketing the bonds to finance the bridge's construction in return for a sizeable commission (Wall, 1970, pp. 270–72). He found a ready market for railroad and bridge company bonds in Europe through the investment bank of Junius S. Morgan in London. This was one result of the fact that, in the late nineteenth century, "falling returns on investments in Europe and low interest rates in the 1870s and 1880s drove European capital to seek higher returns in developing countries such as the United States where investors encountered lies, deception, fraud, and large and repeated defaults" (White, 2011, p. 380). Besides Morgan, Carnegie later used (or attempted to use) Baring Brothers in London and the Sulzbach Brothers in Frankfurt to market bridge and railroad bonds for American companies. Although Carnegie got his commissions and the investment bankers got their profits from the discount on the par value of the bonds they marketed, the European investors lost their shirts when the

Illinois and St. Louis Bridge Company and various American railroads whose bonds they had bought went bankrupt.[18]

Another bridge across the Mississippi constructed by the Keystone Bridge Company in the early 1870s was the Keokuk-Hamilton Bridge, north of St. Louis between Illinois and Iowa. Carnegie and his associates, including Scott and Thomson, were also partners in the Iowa Contracting Company, which built a railroad from Keokuk to Nebraska City, there to link up with lines that connected with the Union Pacific Railroad at Fort Kearney (Wall, 1970, p. 279). Although Keystone did not construct the bridge across the Mississippi connecting Rock Island, Illinois, with Davenport, Iowa, Carnegie and his usual PRR partners, plus some new ones, organized the Davenport and St. Paul Construction Company to build the railroad connecting Davenport with St. Paul, Minnesota. An added benefit for Carnegie was that he also arranged the placing of bonds in Germany for the Davenport and St. Paul Railroad Company (Wall, 1970, p. 280). From all these activities, Carnegie profited in several ways. He profited from supplying the iron and steel components of the bridges and railroads, from the construction itself, and from commissions on the marketing of the bonds issued to finance the construction.

One of those bond-placing episodes resulted in Carnegie becoming (briefly) a member of the board of directors of the Union Pacific Railroad, which almost became an extension of the PRR and, therefore, would have been the first railroad that actually traversed the entire country from coast to coast. Hearing from George Pullman in early 1871 that the Union Pacific desperately needed an infusion of $600,000, Carnegie borrowed enough PRR securities from J. Edgar Thomson to provide equity for a loan of that amount. This resulted in Carnegie, Pullman, and Tom Scott being elected to the Union Pacific board—with Scott as board president. In return, the PRR received thirty thousand shares of $3 million face value Union Pacific stock, to be held by Carnegie, with Carnegie, Scott, Pullman, and Thomson having an option to buy at the then-market price.

When the actual market price rose above the option price, Carnegie ordered the sale of all but four hundred of the shares, and then he divvied up the profits from the difference between the option price at which the shares were bought by him and his cohorts and the market price at which they were sold. The other Union Pacific board members were so angered by this action that they voted Scott, Pullman, and Carnegie off the board (Wall, 1970, pp. 286–89). In his autobiography, Carnegie falsely blames Scott for the sale and the resultant expulsion of all three of them from the Union Pacific board and the subsequent loss of PRR influence (Carnegie, 1920, pp. 164–65). Truly, his own words regarding an instance in which he was bested in the sale of other bonds would seem to have personal application here: "Many men can be trusted, but a few need watching" (Carnegie, 1920, p. 166).

There were two other ways in which Andrew Carnegie was able to use his connections with PRR executives to his advantage during this period. The first involved his early investment in the Woodruff Sleeping Car Company in 1858. By 1862, the company faced stiff competition and rampant patent infringement by those competitors. It needed an infusion of financial capital to expand and legally protect its patents. Carnegie, with the aid of several new Pittsburgh and Philadelphia investors, as well as Scott and Thomson, reorganized the company as the Central Transportation Company and gained majority control. The greatest threat came from George Pullman in Chicago, who had not only copied Woodruff's designs but also improved and refined them.

Central Transportation had franchises with several railroads to supply its sleeping cars, but it greatly coveted a contract with the Union Pacific. Prolonged negotiations between Carnegie, Pullman, and the Union Pacific over several years had two final results. First, in 1867, a contract was signed that created the Pullman Pacific Car Company to supply cars to the Union Pacific. Its joint ownership included stockholders of the Union Pacific, George Pullman, and Carnegie and his associates. The second result was that, in 1870, Carnegie was able to arrange for the Pullman Palace Car Company to lease the assets of the Central Transportation Company in perpetuity for an annual payment of $264,000 (Wall, 1970, pp. 199–208).

Another way Carnegie used his PRR connections is illustrated in his organization of the Keystone Telegraph Company in April 1867. He obtained the right from the PRR to use the railroad's poles in Pennsylvania to run two wires across the state. Using this as leverage, Carnegie and his associates— including David Brooks, his former telegraph office supervisor, and his boyhood friend (and later western division PRR employee), David McCargo— merged his company in a stock swap with rival Pacific and Atlantic Telegraph Company under the latter's name, tripling Keystone Telegraph's asset value in only six months. He then began a rapid expansion of the merged companies and within two years had lines connecting New York, St. Louis, and New Orleans. Under pressure from the competition of Western Union, Carnegie began negotiating with that firm for a stock swap that would merge his company into Western Union. The end result was that Carnegie and his closest associates, including PRR president J. Edgar Thomson, early on exchanged their company's stocks for those of Western Union at a rate of six P & A shares for one Western Union share. Unfortunately for other investors in P & A, the Panic of 1873 disadvantaged latecomers to the deal by driving down the value of Western Union shares. Those other P & A investors were no doubt greatly relieved when Western Union finally absorbed Pacific and Atlantic in 1874 for an annual lease payment of $80,000 (Wall, 1970, pp. 213–20).

Chapter Five

A Man of Steel

In the eighteenth century, Britain encouraged the production of pig and bar iron in its American colonies because of their extensive forests and consequently abundant firewood.[1] The wood was processed into charcoal, which was then used with lime to smelt iron ore into iron. Thus, the American ironmaking industry began as a source of raw material for England's forges and rolling mills. After 1750, coke (coal cake) made from coal displaced charcoal in British iron works, although not in colonial ones—again, because of wood's very abundance there. Coke would not displace charcoal in iron making in North America until almost the middle of the nineteenth century (Taussig, 1931, pp. 47–48).

After the North American British colonies declared independence from Great Britain and won their war to become self-governing states, the newly constituted federal government of the United States sought revenue to fund its operations. The Tariff Act of 1789 taxed imports as a source of that revenue while also imposing special taxes as a means of raising the prices of certain imports, iron and iron products among them. This was done in order to stimulate the domestic production of the specially taxed goods by protecting their higher-cost domestic manufacture from lower-priced foreign competition. The duty for revenue was an *ad valorem* tax of 5 percent on declared value; the protective duties were higher (Taussig, 1931, p. 14). It was only in the twentieth century, with the legislative adoption of other federal taxation measures, that the revenue function of tariffs lost its importance and the protectionist purpose became dominant.

One obvious rationale for early protectionism—and the one mentioned favorably by Andrew Carnegie—was the "infant industry" argument (Carnegie, 1920, pp. 146–48).[2] In a nutshell, the argument is that protection from foreign competition is necessary in order for a capital-intensive domestic industry—like iron manufacturing—to become established and grow. After it has grown to the point that it has achieved the efficiencies of large-scale production, it presumably will have the same low costs as its foreign competitors and will be price competitive with them. At this point, it will no longer require protection to thrive. The protectionist legislators of 1789 hardly could have expected an infancy of more than one hundred years for iron and steel manufacturing when they initiated a protective tariff for that industry. Protection for the iron and steel industries would exist in various forms and at various levels throughout the nineteenth century and into the twentieth.

Under protection, bar and pig iron production in the United States rose steadily in the early nineteenth century—especially during the years of the War of 1812. The peace following the end of the war adversely affected the industry, as well as leaving the federal government with a war debt to pay. The political result was the Tariff of 1816, which imposed an average tax rate of 20 percent on declared values of imports. Special duties were imposed on pig and bar iron imports; the duties were then increased in 1818, as well as extended to iron castings, anchors, nails and spikes (Taussig, 1931, pp. 50–51). With very few exceptions, duties on iron products increased steadily during the first half of the century until, by 1840, prices in the United States were 40–100 percent higher for various domestically made iron products than what it would cost to buy them abroad (Taussig, 1931, p. 55). Obviously, this infant had little incentive to mature, and it raised its prices in tandem with import duties.

Perhaps realizing the historically proven irrelevance of the "infant industry" argument for iron industry tariffs, protectionists of the mid-nineteenth century (with the prominent exception of Carnegie) shifted to the argument that import controls were necessary to "protect the American labor force from cheap foreign labor" (Taussig, 1931, p. 65). Not surprisingly, that simple-minded argument is still the mainstay of protectionist advocacy today.[3] It is simpleminded because the only way to "protect" domestic labor from "cheap foreign labor" would be to prohibit all imports. The longevity of the argument is not surprising because protectionism and nationalism are ideological allies. Protectionists use nationalism as a cover for their rent-seeking activities, while nationalists use protectionist arguments to bolster their chauvinism.

At the root of both doctrines is the erroneous belief of seventeenth-century mercantilists, in service to the politically conflicted nation-states of their day, that one nation's gain is necessarily another nation's loss. Extending this political doctrine to economic relations between trading individuals separated by political borders either ignores or rejects the principle that free exchanges occur because parties to them believe the exchanges to be personally beneficial. Otherwise, it is difficult to understand why they would take place. Trading is an indirect means of accomplishing personal goals. [4]

If both parties to a free exchange benefit, then trade is not a zero-sum game—it produces an increase in economic value for all those who choose to trade with one another. Protectionism prevents this from happening, although the protected industries gain at the expense of the broader society. In that sense, it is protectionism that creates a zero-sum game. Neo-mercantilistic arguments and nationalism remain common political coinage half a millennium later. Advocates of both benefit from this intellectual malaise, as do the protected industries.

By 1860, duties on pig iron were 24 percent. The protectionist Morrill Tariff of 1861 increased them, as did successive revenue tariff acts during the war (Taussig, 1931, pp. 160–66). It was in the context of the protective tariffs that benefited the domestic iron industry that Andrew Carnegie made his first investments in that industry in the early 1860s. [5] This protection was to continue throughout the rest of the century as he and his partners battled their way to preeminence in domestic iron and steel manufacturing, making outsize profits and accumulating their vast fortunes at the expense of other industries and consumers along the way.

The tariffs on iron and steel, and iron and steel products, restricted the supply side of metal markets to the advantage of domestic iron and steel industry investors, owners, and employees during the second half of the nineteenth century. The demand side of those markets was driven primarily by the railroads, which were heavily promoted and subsidized by governments at all levels. [6] The federal government's Pacific Railway acts of 1862 and 1864 created a structure of loans, loan guarantees, and land grants that fueled transcontinental railroad building and stimulated the construction of feeder lines to transcontinental traffic. In 1865, total mileage of railroad track in the United States was 35,085; eight years later, in 1873, it had more than doubled to 70,784 (White, 2011, pp. 17 and 50).

The 1862 act established the Union Pacific Railroad, while that of 1864 underwrote the issuance of bonds so that both the Union Pacific and the Central Pacific could obtain the cash to build.[7] Basically, what happened in both the iron and the railroad industries during this period of expansion was that the government was used as a means of socializing costs while privatizing profits. Canals, banks, and railroads had been subsidized by the states in the 1820s and 1830s and, except for the Erie Canal, proved to be financial disasters. As a result, state subsidies gave way to federal ones as transportation was built ahead of demand for the rest of the century (White, 2011, p. xxvi). On the losing end were consumers, bond buyers, and other industries.

By 1866, the enterprises of Carnegie and his partners included the Freedom Iron Company (reorganized that year as the Freedom Iron and Steel Company), the Union Iron Mills (reorganized as Carnegie, Kloman & Company in 1868), the Keystone Bridge Company, the Superior Rail Mill, and the Pennsylvania Locomotive Works. His Freedom Iron and Steel Company was producing a limited amount of steel with the Bessemer process by 1868, although steel was still too expensive to use to replace iron rails on a widespread basis.[8] The Bessemer process required iron ore with a very low phosphorus content; providentially, ore from the Iron Mountain in the upper Michigan peninsula was tested in 1868 and found to be of that quality (Wall, 1970, pp. 259–66). Added to Carnegie's access to large quantities of low-cost iron ore suitable for the Bessemer process was the proximity of his enterprises to the Connellsville region of southwestern Pennsylvania. The bituminous coal mined in that area produced coke that was superior to that produced elsewhere (Temin, 1964, p. 74). Although Pittsburgh had many local industries, at this point in time it was "mainly an importing and distributing point" (Casson, 1907, p. 87). Carnegie and his partners were now in a position to make it an iron and steel manufacturing center.

In 1867, Andrew Carnegie opened an office in New York City and began living in luxury hotels there. While his brother Tom remained in Pittsburgh, their mother would move to the city and live with Andrew, an arrangement that would continue until her death in 1886. Besides pursuing his business activities in what was becoming the business and financial center of the country, Carnegie began to mix with certain members of the literary and cultural elite of New York.

Engaging in non-business-related social activities was not a new side of Carnegie's life. As early as his time serving as a messenger boy for the Atlantic and Ohio Telegraph Company, he had used his delivery of telegrams to the Pittsburgh Theater as an opportunity to attend Shakespeare plays and other cultural performances there (Carnegie, 1920, p. 48). This led to a life-long love for Shakespeare in addition to spurring him to study history and political theory. His purpose was to understand better what he considered the superiority of his adopted country's political and social orders over those of the European countries and others around the world.

It was also during that same period, when he was a teenager in Pittsburgh, that he and several of his friends formed a debating society that met regularly in the back of the Phipps cobbler shop to discuss the important social and political issues of the time (Wall, 1970, p. 106). Significantly, Carnegie became an early proponent of equal rights for women as well as a vocal opponent of American slavery, an institution that he deplored and publicly opposed until it was abolished. Later, he would handsomely support the Hampton and Tuskegee Institutes and become a friend for life of Booker T. Washington, eventually including Washington on his private pension list (Wall, 1970, pp. 972–73).

After his move back to Pittsburgh from Altoona in December 1859 to become the superintendent of the western division of the Pennsylvania Railroad, Carnegie and several of his friends became members of the Webster Literary Club, which moved from the discussion of purely literary topics to political ones as the nation edged closer to civil war (Wall, 1970, p. 148). The move out of Pittsburgh to Homewood, Pennsylvania, brought with it the opportunity to mix with Carnegie's socially prominent neighbors, which spurred the ambitious young executive to deepen his understanding of literature and culture and to hone the rough edges of his lower-class origins.

In New York, these opportunities were even greater, and Carnegie soon became an enthusiastic participant in the cultural life of the burgeoning literary and arts center of the East Coast. Perhaps the most important influence of these days came from Mrs. Anne Lynch Botta, in whose literary salon Carnegie became an energetic and voluble participant. It may have been among the celebrities who gathered at her home on Saturday evenings that Carnegie became aware of the writings of Herbert Spencer (1820–1903).[9] Acceptance into the Botta salon soon led to other opportunities to associate with the intellectual elite of New York, most notably through his membership in the Nineteenth Century Club (Wall, 1970, p. 364).

In chapter 25 of his autobiography, Carnegie discusses the influence of reading Spencer and their subsequent personal relationship. There, characterizing himself as Spencer's disciple, Carnegie sums up his understanding in the motto "All is well since all grows better" (Carnegie, 1920, p. 339). He goes on to say that man was created with an instinct to rise to a higher form—that man "inherently" rejects the deleterious and absorbs the "beneficial" after experiencing it. He credits Spencer with having made it possible for him to reject religious dogma and embrace Darwinian evolution.

If there is a more erroneous reading of Spencer's central doctrine than that of Carnegie (and this after having supposedly read, associated with, and corresponded with Spencer for decades), it must exist in the writings of the most simple-minded Social Darwinians. So far as the possibility that Carnegie might have sympathized with some of their more extreme views is concerned, he did found the Cold Stream Harbor Laboratory to support the study of eugenics in 1904. The lead researcher, Charles Davenport, was an admirer of Francis Galton, the "father" of eugenics, and Karl Pearson, who favored state-directed selective breeding of human beings. Davenport was more interested in preventing "dysgenic" breeding (Ridley, 2000, p. 289).

In his *Social Statics* ([1851] 1995, p. 3), Herbert Spencer addressed the question of what rule would best produce human happiness, particularly in a social context. He sought to define and defend a "moral law of society" (Spencer, [1851] 1995, p. 18). Such a code of rules would guide "humanity in its highest conceivable perfection" within "an ideal society" (Spencer, [1851] 1995, p. 36). It was Spencer's conviction that social progress was a spontaneous phenomenon of human adaptation to changing natural, intellectual, and social circumstances. Eventually, civilized man would achieve perfection and in society would follow that moral law (Spencer, [1851] 1995, pp. 54–60). Social law provides social order, and an ideal society would follow the ideal moral law (Spencer, [1851] 1995, p. 40). Meanwhile, such a code of rules would provide an ideal toward which imperfect man could strive.[10]

Assuming that the happiness of individual human beings is the "Divine will," that each must find that happiness through the use of all his or her faculties, and that each lives out his or her life socially, Spencer infers a basic political principle that would provide for individual happiness and social harmony: that "every man may claim the fullest liberty to exercise his faculties compatible with the possession of liberty by every other man" (Spencer, [1851] 1995, p. 69). This social rule then entitles each man with rights of life, liberty, free speech, and the use and exchange of property in pursuit of his individual goals (Spencer, [1851] 1995, pp. 102, 116, 131–32).[11] Positing the existence of an inherent "Moral Sense" in every person, he claims that the right and wrong use of human faculties will become known to all. Each person then possesses an "instinct of personal rights" concerning his own actions, as well as a perception of the rights of others that is informed by Adam Smith's concept of "Sympathy," first identified as "a fellow feeling with the passions of others" in Smith's *Theory of Moral Sentiments* (1759).

Not only does the rule that each has the freedom to pursue his own ends, provided that he does not infringe on the like freedom of others, enable the pursuit of individual happiness in a social context, but it is also an agent of social progress, according to Spencer. He argues that social interaction under such a general rule will reveal those actions that are mutually beneficial and those that are injurious to oneself or to others (Spencer, [1851] 1995, p. 75). Civilized man improves and prospers only as he pursues mutually beneficial actions.

These are important implications of Spencer's basic rule for just social interaction in an imperfect world progressing toward a perfect social state of perfect humankind. One is that government is an institution of imperfect society. As civilization advances toward perfection, government decays and will eventually disappear. It exists because of evil (crime) and employs evil means (violence) (Spencer, [1851] 1995, pp. 14, 186). Social progress implies ever more limited government. A perfected man in a perfected society needs no government. In fact, government can retard, even reverse, progress if it grows in power (Spencer, [1851] 1995, p. 216). Its primary duty is "to uphold the law of equal freedom" (Spencer, [1851] 1995, p. 226). If it tries to do more than that, perhaps in an attempt to provide the happiness that the law of equal freedom leaves each individual to use all his or her faculties to seek, it can retard (or reverse) individual and social progress by introducing conflict (Spencer, [1851] 1995, pp. 251–57).

Thus, the state should not engage in the regulation of commerce or impede it in any way. No bounties are to be conferred or tariffs collected that would favor one man's business over another's. It should not support any religious establishment lest some men be made to unwillingly support the religious activity of others. There should be no state-provided welfare, as this retards the process of human adaptation to changing circumstances by favoring those incapable or less capable of adaptation over those capable or more capable. It also relieves the "painful pressure which is effecting [the] transformation" of less civilized man into more civilized man. State-administered welfare likewise supports the unproductive part of the labor force at the expense of the productive part (Spencer, [1851] 1995, pp. 267–93). So far as voluntary philanthropy is concerned, Spencer finds this unobjectionable so long as it is restricted to "helping men to help themselves" (Spencer, [1851] 1995, p. 291).[12]

Spencer argues that there is no more warrant for the state to administer education than there is for it to feed and clothe the population. Further, public education erodes parental responsibility and empowers the state to dictate educational content, which tends to advance the goals of those in power and stifle innovations in teaching and curriculum (Spencer, [1851] 1995, pp. 304–7). Further, government should neither found nor govern colonies; this act transgresses the rights of the home population as well as those of the colony's population. History is full of examples of the evils of colonization. If, to avoid their repetition, the colony were as self-governed as the home country, then it would no longer be a colony (Spencer, [1851] 1995, p. 320). Nor should government attempt to protect the health of the population beyond suppressing nuisances in order to protect individual rights.

There exists a host of other governmental activities that Spencer argues violate the rights of members of its population by going beyond enforcing the basic law of equal freedom. These include the provision of currency and banking services, of postal services, and of public works. Given the content of the past few paragraphs, it is clear that Spencer's views make him a proponent of classical liberal political theory and laissez-faire economics. The last part of the book moves beyond social statics, the requisites of a perfect society, to the dynamics of its coming into existence. And here there is only a slim summary of human progress from the savage state to that of nineteenth-century Western civilization.

Spencer argues that the socializing process that has made the most advanced countries into Adam Smith's highly differentiated and complex societies of cooperating strangers has been enabled by a decline of physical conflict and war, as well as by the development of sympathy and the moral sense. The more brutal and primitive societies have given way to the more advanced. He says, "The conquest of one people over another has been, in the main, the conquest of the social man over the anti-social man; or, strictly speaking, of the more adapted over the less adapted" (Spencer, [1851] 1995, p. 374). In the advanced societies, there is a higher regard for human life, more personal liberty, and more respect for property rights and truth telling. In the final state of perfection, he says there will be the highest individuation as well as the greatest mutual dependence in the form of the extensive division of labor.

This last reference is followed a few pages later by an equation of his social theory with laissez-faire economic theory and the moral law. Because the moral law, the law of equal freedom, "being the law under which perfect individuation, both of man and society, is achieved; being, therefore, the law of that state toward which creation tends, the law of equal freedom may properly be considered as a law of nature" (Spencer, [1851] 1995, p. 414).

Spencer's *Data of Ethics* (1879) seeks to establish a scientific ethics in the face of a perceived decline in the acceptance of moral codes having religious foundations. He argues that all human conduct is directed at: (1) the preservation of one's life; (2) the preservation of the species, through both reproduction and the struggle within and between species; and (3) inner-species cooperation to mutual benefit (Spencer, 1879, pp. 26–30). The subject of ethics is conduct in society as it becomes more peaceful, more industrial, and more mutually cooperative.

If man's purpose is happiness in life, then he must discover and practice an ethics that produces it. Such an ethics must enable each individual member of society to thrive physically, biologically, and psychologically. Most important, it must provide conduct in society "in such wise that the lives of each and all may be the greatest possible, alike in length and breadth" (Spencer, 1879, p. 163). This can only occur in an industrial society from which militancy and aggression have vanished, and in which there is mutual cooperation in an extensive division of labor. Not only must each not hinder the achievement of chosen ends by others, but each must also actively facilitate the efforts of others. There must be beneficence in addition to justice in human interaction. Men must "help to complete one another's lives" (Spencer, 1879, p. 182).

Spencer claims that social history shows the development of the kind of advanced social state that he envisions. He sees the growth of mutual cooperation and decline of aggression within and between societies (Spencer, 1879, pp. 284–85). Early in the book he says that his "Evolution-Hypothesis" is in harmony with this development and that "evolution becomes the highest possible when the conduct simultaneously achieves the greatest totality of life in self, in offspring, and in fellow men; so here we see that the conduct called good rises to the conduct conceived as best, when it fulfills all three classes of ends at the same time" (Spencer, 1879, p. 37). Important agents in this process of adaptation are the moral sentiments—what Adam Smith termed "Sympathy" (Spencer, 1879, pp. 287–96).

In a collection of essays titled *The Man versus the State* ([1884] 1969), Spencer critiques the progression of statism in the thirty years since his *Social Statics*. There, he had argued for the adoption of the "law of equal freedom" as the basic political principle that would provide individual happiness and social harmony. Now Spencer enumerated and chronicled the various well-intentioned British governmental measures by both Tories and Liberals that had restricted the freedom of individual interaction, thus hampering, and sometimes reversing, social evolution.

These included taxation to provide public education, free libraries, public museums, baths, washhouses, recreational facilities and parks, poor relief, and the founding of colonies (Spencer, [1884] 1969, pp. 15, 24, 115, 207). Also, there are regulations controlling the labor of women and children, compulsory insurance, and protectionist restrictions on free trade that channel resources into less productive uses than would otherwise be the case (Spencer, [1884] 1969, pp. 30, 34, 114, 160). All this requires regulatory agents and means even more increased taxation that restricts individual efforts to improve their lives as they see fit. He terms this advance in state functions as socialistic and a move toward "State-socialism," which is a move toward slavery and a regression to a lower state of social life (Spencer, [1884] 1969, pp. 41–42, 76). He also condemns effective restrictions on entry to certain trades imposed by labor unions, as well as the subordination of the union members to the will of union leaders. These are violations of the rights of workers both within and outside of unions (Spencer, [1884] 1969, pp. 48–49, 73–75).

Given the actual arguments and opinions that Herbert Spencer presented in his various works, how does one assess Andrew Carnegie's assertion that he was Spencer's "disciple"? Against such a claim stand Spencer's opposition to tariffs (which Carnegie supported because they enriched him); Spencer's opposition to public works, such as government-funded bridges (the construction of which also helped build Carnegie's fortune); Spencer's opposition to laws limiting the working conditions of women and children (which Carnegie would publicly advocate); Spencer's opposition to public education (which Carnegie would include in his philanthropic enterprise); Spencer's opposition to taxation-funded free public libraries (which Carnegie would necessitate for any city accepting his donation of a library building); and, lastly, Spencer's strong support for a completely laissez-faire economic regime (elements of which Carnegie only favored when some aspect served his purposes and opposed when it suited him). [13]

To be fair, Carnegie and Spencer were in agreement regarding being advocates of peace and opponents of militancy, war, and colonization. Although he would support the Spanish-American War in 1898, Carnegie strongly opposed occupying the Philippines as an American colony, which occurred after the war's conclusion. Spencer was opposed to effective trade union activities, whereas Carnegie would publicly support their existence but then privately strive to create and operate nonunion plants, most notably before and during the Homestead Strike in 1892. They both opposed slavery and were proponents of industrialization. Even more tellingly, Carnegie would adopt as his guiding philanthropic principle "to help those who will help themselves," the exceptional form of philanthropy that gained Spencer's approval.

Nevertheless, Carnegie's distillation of Spencer's main doctrine of social evolution as "All is well since all grows better" is strongly misrepresentative, especially in view of Spencer's later rejection of any teleology or determinism and his pessimistic conviction that late nineteenth-century government was socially retrogressive in its general effect. Spencer never identified any "instinct" in man to rise to a higher form, and he certainly did not believe that man "inherently" absorbs the beneficial and rejects the deleterious aspects of existence. A "disciple" of Spencer, Carnegie most certainly was not.

In 1882, Carnegie managed to be included in a visit and tour of the eastern United States by Spencer. He arranged to travel on the same ship as Spencer as it sailed to New York from England and to become acquainted with him during the voyage. Their time spent together during Spencer's American tour was deeply disappointing for both men, albeit for different reasons: Spencer found industrial Pittsburgh appalling, and Carnegie was miffed at Spencer's coldness toward him. However, they parted cordially just before Spencer's departure from New York harbor on November 11 and corresponded for years afterward (Wall, 1970, pp. 382–89).

In December 1868, Andrew Carnegie wrote out a statement of his total business holdings and their book values. The value total was $400,000, which had produced an income of $56,110 for the year (Wall, 1970, p. 223). In twenty years he had risen from a thirteen-year-old boy with no assets and an income of $1.20 a week to an independently wealthy thirty-three-year-old man. That month he also wrote out a life plan in the form of a memo to himself that was found in a desk drawer after his death. In the memo, he wrote that in two years he would set aside business affairs and live on an annual income of $50,000. Any surplus would be devoted to philanthropy, while he would pursue studies at Oxford University and a literary and public policy career. He argued to himself that "to continue much longer overwhelmed by business cares and with most of my thoughts wholly upon the way to make more money in the shortest time, must degrade me beyond hope of permanent recovery" (Wall, 1992, p. 41). The philanthropic aspect would be the only part of this plan to be fully realized in the years to come. Carnegie was now positioned to be at the forefront of those about to inaugurate the Age of Steel in America, and he would stay there, however personally degrading it might be for him.

Building bridges kept Keystone Bridge and Carnegie, Kloman & Company profitable through the early 1870s, and selling railroad bonds in Europe earned large commissions for Carnegie; however, he had his eye on a much bigger prize.[14] With the availability of the low-phosphorus iron ore of the Lake Superior region and the high-quality coke made from the coal of the Connellsville area, he decided that it was now possible to use the Bessemer process to produce steel in the quantities needed, and at a low enough cost, to replace iron rails with those made from steel. What was needed was a large enough industrial plant to do this.

Carnegie's old iron master friend and partner in the Columbia Oil Company, William Coleman, was just as convinced as Carnegie that the time had come to build a plant to produce steel in as large quantities as was then being done in England using the Bessemer process. Coleman had obtained an option to buy 106 acres of land in the area twelve miles south of Pittsburgh known as "Braddock's Field."[15] It was bounded on the south by the Monongahela River, which provided a water route to Pittsburgh and convergence with the Allegheny and Ohio rivers. At the northern boundary were the rails of the PRR, and the Baltimore and Ohio Railroad ran through the center of the property (Bridge, 1903, p. 70).[16] To the southeast were the coal fields of Connellsville.

Carnegie put together a partnership of local business acquaintances and friends that included himself, his brother Tom, William Coleman, Andrew Kloman, Henry Phipps Jr., Thomas Scott, J. Edgar Thomson, David McCandless, David Stewart, and John Scott. Stewart was Thomas Scott's nephew, a neighbor of Tom Carnegie and president of both the Pittsburgh Locomotive Works and the Columbia Oil Company, while John Scott was a local banker, an officer in the Pittsburgh, Virginia and Charleston Railroad, and also president of the Allegheny Valley Railroad. McCandless, one of the founders of the local Swedenborgian church along with Will Carnegie and

Andy's aunt Annie Aiken, was an old friend of the family, vice president of the Exchange National Bank, and widely respected in Pittsburgh. Perhaps in recognition of McCandless's prominence in the local community, the new steel company, organized on November 5, 1872, and capitalized at $700,000, was named Carnegie, McCandless & Company. The plant itself was named "The Edgar Thomson Steel Works" (E.T.) in honor of that Carnegie partner and current PRR president.

Carnegie's $250,000 was the largest investment, followed by $100,000 each from Coleman and McCandless, and then $50,000 each from Stewart, John Scott, Tom Carnegie, Phipps, and Kloman. Edgar Thomson and Tom Scott were minor investors who took a part of Carnegie's share (Wall, 1970, p. 309; Nasaw, 2006, p. 143).[17] It is worth noting that four of the ten partners were railroad executives and potential customers of this new steel rail manufacturer.

According to Casson (1907, p. 84), McCandless and Coleman gave the new firm its prestige; Andrew Carnegie, John Scott, and Stewart were to get the orders; and William P. Shinn, a vice president of John Scott's Allegheny Valley Railroad, was the general manager. Phipps was to handle accounting and cost control, Kloman ran the plant, and Tom Carnegie was jack of all trades within the firm.[18] Perhaps the biggest part in fueling their anticipation of a profitable future for the partnership was played by the Tariff Act of 1870. Although it reduced the duty on pig iron from $9 to $7 a ton, it raised the duty on steel rails to $28 a ton (Taussig, 1931, p. 179).[19] Protected by that duty, and producing rails on a large scale in a state-of-the-art plant, they expected to take the domestic market away from the British, as well as from their American competitors.

To design and supervise the building of the new plant, Carnegie chose Alexander L. Holley, an engineer with more than a decade of experience in the designing and building of Bessemer converters.[20] Holley's last project had been the design and installation of the converter at the Cambria Iron Works in Johnstown, Pennsylvania. With him as his chief assistant when he came to Braddock's Field was Captain William R. Jones, formerly assistant to the superintendent of the Cambria works and soon to become invaluable to the E.T. as its first general superintendent. Jones in turn recruited more than two hundred workmen, foremen, and department superintendents from Cambria who were dissatisfied with recent wage cuts there, and he set them to work building the new mill (Wall, 1970, pp. 313–16). It would take almost two years to build before rail production began in the late summer of 1875.

The Panic of 1873 and resultant recession was a financial disaster for some firms, but not for Carnegie, McCandless & Company. The partners had the cash for their subscriptions, and building during a recession meant that materials, labor, and transportation costs were less than in earlier years. Carnegie was able to build the plant for 75 percent of what it otherwise would have cost. He did have to sell some of his shares in other companies, take out short-term loans from McCandless's Exchange Bank and other local banks, and place $400,000 of bonds through Junius Morgan in London. However, as a result of the Panic and recession years following it, he was able to buy out both Tom Scott and Edgar Thomson when they experienced financial difficulties in 1873. He would buy out Kloman and Coleman for the same reason in 1876 (Wall, 1970, pp. 303, 310, 318–19). When David McCandless died in 1878, his shares would be sold back to the company at par, and Andrew Carnegie would become the majority partner at 59 percent of the $1.25 million of invested capital (Hendrick, 1932, vol. 1, p. 214).

Holley's plan for the works included two five-ton Bessemer converters to make the steel and a rolling mill to roll the steel into rails (Wall, 1970, p. 320). Because it would be a new plant, Holley could design the plant around the process of making steel rather than having to fit the process into an available iron-making plant, which had been the case in other works (Misa, 1995, p. 24). The iron for the converters would come from a new blast furnace at the Union Mills, which had previously depended on pig iron from local producers. The new plant also would include two Siemens open-hearth furnaces to make high-grade steel for special orders.[21] In December 1870, the two Carnegies, Kloman, and Phipps had reorganized Union Mills as Carnegie, Kloman & Company and began work on the giant furnace—the "Lucy"—which was completed in 1872.[22] When the E.T. plant was completed, it would have a reliable source of pig iron in sufficient quantities for its converters.

The Bessemer converter process transformed the social dynamics of steel making. Previously, iron and steel making had been craft-based and controlled by the iron workers—particularly the puddlers, who removed the carbon by stirring the molten pig iron to make wrought iron. Afterward, the precise amount of carbon could be added to make steel (Temin, 1964, p. 19). Production was in relatively small amounts, labor intensive, and time consuming. With the giant converters, production would be almost continuous and capital intensive, controlled by metallurgical chemists, engineers, and managers. "Chemistry was the central issue for Holley," and he wanted metallurgical chemists to guide the manufacture of Bessemer steel (Misa, 1995, p. 30).[23] This set the stage for conflict on several levels because it was also now possible to hire relatively unskilled labor and train it for the steel-making process, pitting craft against noncraft as well as labor against management.

Although Holley estimated the cost of producing rails using the new plant at $69 a ton and expected the average price of rails to remain at the current price of $100 a ton, so that at an output of 30,000 tons a year the plant would almost pay for itself in its first year of operation, both costs and prices turned out to be less. Nevertheless, E.T. earned $11,000 profit in its first month of operation and ultimately proved to be even more profitable than Holley had expected (Hendrick, 1932, vol. 1, p. 200).[24] The first order for two thousand steel rails came from the PRR on August 6, 1875. Despite the name of the works, every steel rail produced at Braddock's Field had "Carnegie" stamped on it (Hendrick, 1932, vol. 1, p. 287).

The major American steel makers had formed the Bessemer Steel Association (BSA) in June 1875, "for the exchange of information and the promotion of lobbying activities to support favorable tariff legislation" (Wall, 1970, p. 330). Shinn had attended that organizational meeting, and a year later, when the BSA held a meeting in Philadelphia to form a pooling agreement to divide up the market, set prices, and assign production quotas, it was Andrew Carnegie who attended.[25] When it was apparent that his firm would be assigned the lowest quota, the brash young newcomer told the assembled members that he knew their costs of production and his firm's were lower. If he was not given the same quota as the largest assigned to any firm, he would undersell them all. Carnegie got his way then and in future years, participating in pooling arrangements when it suited him and breaking these price and production agreements when it was more profitable for him to do so (Wall, 1970, p. 332).

Andrew Carnegie had two basic managerial obsessions. The first was cost minimization. He knew his competitors' costs, but, because his ownership model was a closely held partnership, his competitors didn't know his.[26] He constantly worked to reduce his production costs below theirs, carefully scrutinizing the costs of all inputs and every aspect of the production process in his factories.[27] This made it possible not only to increase his profit margins in good times but also to preserve the power to reduce prices when it was necessary to keep the orders coming in. The ability to do so was particularly important during recession years, when Carnegie would cut prices to keep production up at low profit rates rather than lose sales, cut production, and lay off workers (Nasaw, 2006, pp. 174–76).

Cost minimization did not mean quality minimization; Carnegie always strove to increase the quality of his products using the latest techniques and processes. That made it possible to compete on a quality basis when he wasn't competing on price. Yet, in speaking of what it is that makes a firm a lasting one in his autobiography, he says, "The surest foundation of a manufacturing concern is quality [and] after that, and a long way after, comes cost" (Carnegie, 1920, p. 123).

Cost reduction sometimes took unusual forms, as shown in the following example: Henry Phipps was constantly on the lookout for unnoticed opportunities. He discovered that flue cinder from furnaces and scale (steel shavings) from rolling mills were treated as waste by other iron and steel plants, although both could be reused in the steel-making production process. The flue cinder was a blast furnace by-product, which scale was for rolling mills. The E.T. management was able to keep this trade secret for years, buying both by-products from Union Mills competitors for much less than the cost of iron ore—that is, until those competitors finally realized what Phipps was doing (Bridge, 1903, p. 64; Wall, 1970, p. 342). Perhaps because of his dedication to Carnegie and his success at cost-cutting, Phipps was the only early Carnegie partner who was still with him when Carnegie Steel was sold and became part of U.S. Steel.

Carnegie's second obsession was restricting partners' salaries and dividends in order to retain and use profits for capital investment.[28] This provided the funds for innovation, expansion, and adoption of the latest techniques and equipment—particularly during recessions, when other firms were simply fighting to stay afloat. His rationale was that "a manufacturing concern in a growing country like ours begins to decay when it stops extending" (Carnegie, 1920, p. 226). This policy caused friction between him and his partners, several of whom—including his own brother—would have preferred more money over the rising capital value of the firm; however, as the majority partner, Carnegie had his way. He argued, "The men who have succeeded are men who have chosen one line and stuck to it. It is surprising how few men appreciate the enormous dividends derivable from investment in their own business . . . unless the business will not bear extension" (Carnegie, 1920, p. 177).

In contrast to his competitors, Carnegie used the closely held partnership form of business organization. The number of partners was strictly limited.

In his opinion, this "association" of partners had several advantages over the widely held public corporation organization. For one thing, partnerships were not required to make public their internal business plans and performance information. By purchasing a few public shares in his incorporated competitors, Carnegie was able to get their annual reports while they could only know what he would tell them about his company's internal affairs—unless, of course, they followed his practice of clandestinely obtaining information from his competitors' employees or business associates. Another advantage, according to Carnegie, was faster decision making (Carnegie, 1920, p. 221). Of course, with him as the majority partner, decision making had to be faster—especially if he disagreed with his partners.

A still greater advantage of Carnegie's system was that partners had a strong interest in the success of their own business because "the company's success was the [partner] manager's success, and the able manager could not leave without losing his interest in the future growth of the company" (Wall, 1970, p. 328). Reinvesting profits in the firm, instead of increasing salaries or distributing profits, grew it that much faster, increased the potential value of ownership shares, and increased the incentive to work harder to be more productive. Furthermore, Carnegie's partnership agreements valued shares at par for buybacks, and partners who left would not be able to take with them any increased capital value created by those reinvested profits. In effect, they were bound to the firm at their original investment until Carnegie chose to recapitalize. If they left before that, Carnegie could buy them out for less than the market-estimated value of their capital investment.

Another advantage of the partnership form was that it provided a strong incentive for ambitious employees who were not yet partners to earn Carnegie's attention by performing well. As he said himself, "There is no way of making a business successful that can vie with the policy of promoting those who render exceptional service" (Carnegie, 1920, p. 201). He tended to add new partners from top-performing employees within his firms as they grew, and his employees knew this. They also knew that it was his practice that they pay for their partnership shares out of their dividends, rather than in cash up front. Many of his top managers had originally started as unskilled or semiskilled labor. They rose from jobs as clerks, water boys, office boys, rollers, messenger boys, and unskilled laborers. A prime example is Charles Schwab, originally employed as a rodman at $1 a day, who would not only arrange the eventual deal with J. P. Morgan that merged Carnegie Steel with other firms to form U.S. Steel in 1901 but also become the first president of that giant corporation.[29]

In addition to the advantages he gained from the partnership form of ownership, Carnegie had as keen an eye for recognizing talent in employees and associates as he did in recognizing and adopting innovations in business practices and production methods.[30] Of course, some of them—like the Dodd or Webb processes of grafting steel facings onto iron rails—failed, but that didn't stop him. He was a risk taker despite his assertion that "pioneering doesn't pay a new concern" (Casson, 1907, p. 82). He carefully chose his partners from among boyhood friends, trusted and ambitious relatives, businessmen associates or neighbors, references from men whose judgment he trusted, and employees within his firms. Like his experience with innovations in production methods, a few, like Tom Miller or the Kloman brothers, didn't work out as well as he had anticipated.

Nevertheless, Andrew Carnegie was a shrewd judge of men, business practices, and general business trends. After he relocated his main residence to New York City in 1867 and later opened an office in the financial district, he spent much time and effort keeping up with the latest business and economic news.[31] The business and information center of the country was a good place to be to formulate future plans and strategies (Wall, 1970, p. 351). He also was determined to produce a quality product at all times and, as has been mentioned before, was intimately knowledgeable about the latest techniques and practices particular to his industries.

When Andrew Kloman left the firm, Carnegie, Kloman & Company was reorganized as Carnegie Brothers. When Coleman was forced to sell out, Carnegie, McCandless & Company was reorganized as the Edgar Thomson Steel Company, Ltd., with the capitalization increased to $1 million.[32] After McCandless's death, the capitalization was increased to $1.25 million with Andrew Carnegie as the majority partner. Finally, conflicts between Carnegie and William P. Shinn led to Shinn's departure from E.T. Steel and an opportunity for further consolidation.

In April 1881, Carnegie Brothers, the Edgar Thomson Steel Company, and a number of Carnegie's other iron- and steel-production-related firms were merged and reorganized as Carnegie Brothers & Company, Ltd. Partners were Andrew and Tom Carnegie, Henry Phipps Jr., David Stewart, John Scott, John W. Vandevort, and Gardner McCandless (David McCandless's son and former personal secretary to Andrew Carnegie). Capitalization was now $5 million, Tom Carnegie was board chairman, Andrew Carnegie held the majority interest, and profits that year were $2 million, or 40 percent return on invested capital (Wall, 1970, pp. 357–60). The stage was now set for vigorous expansion.

Domestic steel rail prices were $170 a ton in 1867; by 1880, they had fallen to $70 a ton. The trend was downward for the next five years to $30 in 1885 (Misa, 1995, p. 32). The British prices in the low $30s during the same period, plus the $28 per ton duty, acted to keep out British rails except for the most expansionist years of railroad construction.[33] As purchasers of steel rails, the railroads would be expected to oppose the tariffs; however, as shown by the example of the Carnegie partners, there was a community of interests between the rail producers and the rail purchasers. As Temin (1964, p. 174) comments, "As long as the costs to the railroad of new rails could be passed on to the [transportation] consumer, there was no reason to balk at higher prices if they facilitated the growth of an industry in which the railroads were also involved." And they could be passed on with corrupt state legislatures setting rail rates to ensure "a reasonable profit" and railroad executives as partners in their rail suppliers. Pockets could be filled on both sides of the rail market, at the expense of other industries and rail shippers and passengers.

Carnegie Brothers had added a second "Lucy" furnace in 1877, and E.T. was then producing more rails than any mill in the United States. Two more blast furnaces were built at the Braddock's Field plant a few years later to increase production even more (Wall, 1970, p. 346). Meanwhile, Captain Jones was constantly replacing machinery and improving it.[34] One of his inventions was the "Jones Mixer," a brick-lined iron box that could hold the output of several blast furnaces, thus mixing and homogenizing the molten iron before it was poured into the Bessemer converters (Misa, 1995, p. 27).

Jones had five operating principles: employ young and ambitious men, mix nationalities in the workforce, use the most up-to-date machinery, encourage competition between plants, and reduce the workday from twelve to eight hours to make labor more productive (Casson, 1907, pp. 27–28).[35] Only the last item met opposition from Carnegie, although he finally agreed to it for the E.T. works. The experiment lasted ten years, except for a period of low demand and prices for steel in 1885 (Wall, 1970, pp. 520, 527; Nasaw, 2006, pp. 259–62).

Carnegie's E.T. works had produced more steel than could be rolled into rails in the late 1870s, and he sold the extra to local manufacturers to be made into other steel products. Expansion of rail production brought an end to this sale of excess ingots, and so Solar Iron Works owner William Clark and six other Pittsburgh ironmasters—including Andrew Kloman—incorporated the Pittsburg Bessemer Steel Company in October 1879, intending to produce their own steel for rolling rails and structural material.[36] They bought land and built a new Bessemer steel works down the river from the E.T. works at Homestead, a small town on the south bank of the Monongahela with a direct rail link to Pittsburgh.

Their new plant and a glass factory built the same year became the industrial nucleus of a growing suburb of the booming city to the north. Although prevented from licensing the Bessemer patents by the Bessemer Steel Association, the owners of Pittsburg Bessemer were able to obtain the help of Alexander Holley to design around the patents. The downside of the resultant unique plant was that it created a workforce with skills specific to that plant. This would turn out to be a major factor favorable to the labor side in Pittsburg Bessemer's conflicts with its workforce in the years to come (Krause, 1992, p. 170).

Soon Pittsburg Bessemer was a viable rival to Carnegie's firm and a threat to his expansion (Wall, 1970, pp. 474–76). This was not to last, for, in addition to his partnership in the firm, William Clark was the Homestead plant manager, and his efforts to lower wages and force workers to follow rigid work rules stimulated his skilled workers to become members of the Amalgamated Association of Iron and Steel Workers.[37] There were periodic clashes between its members and Clark's management that finally resulted in a violent strike in early 1882—a strike that presaged in its details, if not its level of violence, the strike at Homestead in 1889, as well as the infamously violent Homestead Strike three years after that.

Clark had closed the mill on January 1, 1882, and told the workers that to be reemployed they must sign an agreement by January 5 not to join the union or to strike for higher wages. The skilled workforce refused to sign. For the next three months there were periodic brawls and shootouts between striking steel workers, on one side, and police, sheriff's deputies, replacements hired by Clark, and plant guards, on the other. Lacking the workforce to work the unique mill, production at Pittsburg Bessemer virtually halted. Union leaders formed an advisory committee to coordinate the strike and took over the town. On March 4, members of the Amalgamated Association voted in favor of sympathy strikes at the mills of the other partners of Pittsburg Bessemer. Facing this threat, the mill owners capitulated to the union, and work at Homestead resumed on March 20. Clark resigned nine days later (Krause, 1992, pp. 174–91).

A decline in rail demand in 1883, coupled with more problems with the union, led to the forced sale that fall of the entire Homestead works to Carnegie Brothers at the value of the original investment (Wall, 1970, pp. 486–88). Carnegie got a new plant without having to build it, and the owners got out with their financial skins intact.

By 1886, Homestead had been converted to rolling steel plates and structural steel beams instead of rails. Again, Carnegie's entrepreneurial alertness to future opportunities showed itself, as the market for structural steel products grew rapidly during the 1880s, while the growth in rail production lagged far behind (Nasaw, 2006, p. 247). He had also arranged the merger of the Lucy Furnaces with Pittsburg Bessemer to form Carnegie, Phipps & Company. Carnegie was now majority partner in two steel companies— Carnegie Brothers and Carnegie, Phipps—and he was rolling not only rails for the expanding railroads but also structural steel beams, which would become increasingly important as cities began to replace masonry construction of buildings with those having steel skeletons. The Age of the Skyscraper was about to begin, and Andrew Carnegie had the entrepreneurial insight to see this.

Carnegie's Union Mills already had been rolling I-beams capable of twenty-foot spans, but with the conversion of the Homestead plant to the production of a variety of structural shapes, it was now ready to become a supplier to Chicago building contractors. As Chicago School architect Louis Sullivan relates in his autobiography, the problem posed by the limits of masonry construction of buildings was solved by engineers of eastern rolling mills that were rolling bridge structural shapes. At that time, Chicago's rolling mills were rolling only steel rails, while the city's architects—taking their cue from railroad bridge design—were designing buildings with skeletons of structural steel (Misa, 1995, p. 50). Here was an opportunity for Carnegie's entrepreneurial alertness and pioneering spirit to steal a march on local rolling mills.

The first steel-framed skyscraper in Chicago, designed by William Jenney, was built in the mid-1880s.[38] The construction superintendent of the nine-story Home Insurance Building was a bridge designer, and the contract for the structural shapes went to Carnegie's company in 1884. As Misa (1995, p. 60) puts it, "With this effort Carnegie Steel placed itself at the center of Chicago building at a providential moment." It was certainly providential for the architects—they needed a knowledgeable supplier for the skeletons of their buildings—and it was providential for Carnegie in that he needed customers for structural steel to supplant the falling demand for steel rails.

One of Carnegie's bridge engineers, Charles L. Strobel, who had been employed at Keystone Bridge from 1878 to 1885, was sent to Chicago in 1886 as a consulting engineer for the architectural firm of (Dankmar) Adler and (Louis) Sullivan (Misa, 1995, p. 65). The result was that Carnegie, Phipps supplied the heavy structural steel shapes for Adler and Sullivan's path-breaking Auditorium Building, while Keystone Bridge supplied the trusses and other components of the theater, which was completed in 1889 (Misa, 1995, pp. 47–48). Perhaps it was Carnegie's entrepreneurial example that caused Chicago's Union Iron, North Chicago Rolling Mill, and Joliet Iron and Steel to merge into Illinois Steel in 1889 and begin making structural shapes.[39]

Carnegie also never stopped pushing for greater sales, as well as quality improvements in his structural steel products, despite his participation in a beam pool from 1885 to 1892 to prevent price rivalry. Seventeen of the twenty-nine classic Chicago School buildings built in the period 1885–1895 were built with Carnegie's steel columns and beams. He and Captain Jones worked to increase the length and improve the shape of beams, which made his firm's beams technically superior to those of his competitors, while Charles Strobel wrote a company handbook that became the standard of the industry (Misa, 1995, pp. 70–74). Misa is right on the mark when he says, "In the midst of technical uncertainty, Carnegie Steel had seized the moment."

Meanwhile, Carnegie had entered into a business relationship that would prove to be the most momentous of his career. Coke was a key ingredient of iron and steel making. The anthracite coal of eastern Pennsylvania contained very little impurities and was viewed as a natural coke. Coke also could be made by heating the softer bituminous coal and cooking the impurities out of it. The bituminous coal of the Connellsville region of western Pennsylvania made a superior coke because the production process left it honeycombed with pockets that gave more surface area for burning. This made for faster burning than could be achieved with the denser anthracite, and thus faster pig iron production (Temin, 1964, p. 158). The king of Connellsville coke was Henry Clay Frick, whose Henry C. Frick Coke Company had first incorporated in 1871 and grew to own three thousand acres of coal deposits and more than one thousand coke ovens of the Connellsville region by 1882

(Warren, 1996, p. 15). Born December 19, 1849, in modest circumstances, Frick had become a millionaire by the time he was thirty years old through investing in coal fields and coke ovens.

Carnegie saw in Frick an opportunity to secure a talented managing partner and assured coke supply for his furnaces. He was already Frick's major customer. Frick must have seen in Carnegie the opportunity of assured production demand as well as increased financial resources for expansion (Warren, 1996, p. 29). In early 1882, by mutual agreement, the Henry C. Frick Coke Company was reorganized with a capitalization of $2 million and Carnegie Brothers as a minority partner.[40] During the next two years, Carnegie steadily increased his percentage of the partnership until, by December 1883, Carnegie Brothers had become the majority partner, while Frick retained operational control. Frick's expansion in the production of coke now fed Carnegie's expansion of rail and structural steel, a vital step in what would later become the vertical integration of the steel-making process (Wall, 1970, pp. 485–86). By 1887, Frick had expanded to five thousand ovens and was producing six thousand tons of coke a day (Harvey, 1928, p. 82).

A last threat to Carnegie's dominance of the steel industry in the Pittsburgh area arose in 1885, when another group of businessmen and manufacturers organized the Duquesne Steel Company and began to construct a plant a few miles up the river from both Homestead and Braddock's Field. Reincorporated as the Allegheny Bessemer Steel Company, it introduced innovations that significantly reduced the costs of producing steel rails. Carnegie's response was to send circulars to railroads claiming that the rails produced by the new methods lacked "homogeneity of structure" (Wall, 1970, p. 498). He also got the members of the Bessemer Steel Association to exclude the new firm from the rail pool (Casson, 1907, p. 113). The combination of those two measures, plus labor problems at the plant, put the company in a precarious financial position in the fall of 1889 and through the following year.

By then Frick had become an 11 percent partner and chairman of Carnegie Brothers & Company. He and Carnegie were of one mind on eliminating the competition. Late in 1890, Frick offered the owners of the Allegheny $1 million in Carnegie Brothers bonds to sell out to Carnegie Brothers, which they accepted. With new ownership now running a mill producing rails that had previously lacked "homogeneity of structure," the flaw miraculously disappeared and the plant generated a profit equivalent to its purchase price in its first year of operation (Casson, 1907, p. 113). Carnegie quickly introduced the new process at Homestead and the E.T. works, thus giving the lie to any suspicions he had voiced concerning its efficacy (Wall, 1970, p. 499).

It was also during the early 1880s that Carnegie's alert entrepreneurial eye fell upon the solution to another key problem of the steel-making process, and he pushed strongly for its adoption in America. An English amateur chemist named Sidney Gilchrist-Thomas had discovered a method for removing the phosphorus from iron by mixing lime with it at a very high temperature. The phosphorus would bind to the lime to make slag, while the Bessemer process turned the iron into steel. This made it possible to use high-phosphorus iron in a Bessemer converter, although it required a special "basic lining" to withstand the resultant heat. Alexander Holley read Gilchrist-Thomas's paper on the process and sent it to mining and metallurgical engineer George W. Maynard, who arranged a successful test of the process in England in 1879. When Carnegie learned of the process and its successful trial, he pushed the Bessemer Steel Association to buy the patent rights from Gilchrist-Thomas and an American named Jacob Reese, who had independently made the same discovery (Wall, 1970, pp. 500–504).

Unfortunately, results varied from one manufacturer to another, depending on how careful each was in applying the Gilchrist-Thomas/Reese process, and many switched back to using low-phosphorus ore. But Carnegie became aware in 1885 that British firms had found the new process worked even better in Siemens open-hearth furnaces, and he already had two of them at Braddock's Field. So, he ordered more, and by the fall of 1888 several open-hearth furnaces were in operation at Homestead and two more had been ordered for the E.T. works. What this episode shows about Carnegie's farsightedness is best said by Wall:

> Even though Carnegie had hundreds of thousands of dollars invested in Bessemer converters, he was ready to scrap them in favor of a better and more economical process. Construction costs never bothered Carnegie. It was operational cost that mattered, and that simple truth was a major reason for his success.[41] (Wall, 1970, p. 505)

The fall of 1886 was a serious low point in Andrew Carnegie's personal life. He contracted typhoid fever and nearly died, his alcoholic brother Tom developed pneumonia and died in October, and their ailing mother died on November 10. The business implications of the death of Tom and near-death of Andrew greatly alarmed Henry Phipps. The partnership agreement would have required Carnegie Brothers and Carnegie, Phipps to buy back Tom's and Andrew's shares immediately at par if both brothers had died, and this would have meant bankruptcy for both companies. So Phipps had a new partnership agreement drawn up for all partners to sign that provided for buybacks to occur over an extended period of time, to be determined by the ownership percentage being bought. This "Iron Clad" agreement also stipulated that if three-fourths of the partners owning three-fourths of the value of shares requested it, any partner could be forced to sell his interest back to the company at par (Wall, 1970, pp. 490–93).

The new agreement not only protected the company from the consequences of a major partner's demise but also strengthened Carnegie's hold over the other partners because of his majority interest. It obviously exempted him from its provision for a forced sale, and it did one thing more: it practically guaranteed that the price paid in a forced sale would be below the expected market value of the shares since Carnegie never overcapitalized his firms—rather, the opposite was true (Nasaw, 2006, p. 288).

Both Captain Jones and Henry Frick had supported Carnegie in the company's investment in open-hearth furnaces and the change of direction away from sole reliance on the Bessemer process. Jones did so because he was always in favor of using the latest equipment, machinery, and production processes; Frick did so because he agreed with Carnegie that reinvestment of profits to decrease costs and increase the capital value of the firm was the best long-run strategy (Wall, 1970, p. 506). Unfortunately, Jones died on September 28, 1889, as a result of a furnace explosion two days earlier, and the outcome of the Homestead Strike of 1892 would drive a wedge between Carnegie and Frick that eventually led to the dissolution of their managerial partnership and Frick's exit from management. Because of overlooked problems in the three "Iron Clad" agreements drawn up over the years, this would prove to be unexpectedly contentious and favorable to Frick, much to Carnegie's dismay.

After Jones's death, twenty-seven-year-old Charles Schwab was promoted from superintendent of the Homestead plant to Jones's position at the E.T., and Frick proposed that Carnegie Brothers and Carnegie, Phipps be combined into one steel-making firm.[42] The merger of the two firms into Carnegie Steel Company, Ltd., finally took place July 1, 1892, with a capitalization of $25 million, a majority holding by Carnegie of 55.33 percent, and Henry Clay Frick as board chairman (Wall, 1970, p. 536).[43] The birth of Carnegie Steel would be one under fire because it coincided with a lockout and subsequent strike of all workers at the Homestead plant that very quickly led to violence, several deaths, and the final intervention of the Pennsylvania state militia.

The illness and death of Mag Carnegie in November 1886 did have one very positive effect on Andrew Carnegie's personal life—it opened the path to marriage for him. At this time he was fifty-three years old and still unmarried. This was not because he was uninterested in the opposite sex or too busy for courtship. Rather, it was the possessiveness of his mother that was the main barrier to any courtship that might lead to marriage. It is to be recalled that it was his mother who was the real head of the Carnegie household. It was she who opened a grocery business and sewed shoes for her brother Tom in Dunfermline when Will Carnegie's weaving income dropped precipitately. It was she who wrote her twin sisters inquiring about the job situation in America for years after their emigration in 1840. It was no doubt she who made the decision for the Carnegie family to emigrate and join her sisters and their families in 1848 when the Carnegie family's financial situation became so dire (Wall, 1970, pp. 65–78).

Once in Pittsburgh, and faced with Will's unwillingness to abandon his weaving and work at another trade, Mag bound shoes for Henry Phipps Sr. to support the family. She also worked Saturdays in her sister Annie's grocery store in Allegheny City while Will continued to weave and futilely attempt to sell his cloths. Mag Carnegie was fiercely proud and protective of both her sons, and it was no doubt she who urged young Andy to interview for the telegraph office job when Will was doubtful of any likely success (Carnegie, 1920, p. 33). It was also her influence that encouraged Andrew's religious skepticism (Wall, 1970, p. 129).

In addition, Mag Carnegie may have been the dominant outside influence driving Andrew Carnegie's career ambitions. Recall that she even mortgaged her home to provide funds so that he could repay the balance due on the loan that enabled his first business investment. Besides tributes to her honor, courage, and strength of character that appear in several places in his autobiography, he also notes that his first published book contains the dedication "To my favorite Heroine—My Mother" (Carnegie, 1920, p. 6).

Given that background, and the fact that his mother joined him when he moved to Altoona in 1858 and continued to move, travel, and live with him until her death, it is almost certain that their closeness was a suppressing factor for any serious open courtship. Nonetheless, this did not prevent Andrew Carnegie from publicly socializing with women, and even becoming close friends with some of them.

While he acted as Tom Scott's assistant in Altoona in the late 1850s after Scott's promotion to general superintendent of the PRR, for recreation Andy learned to ride horses and drive carriages. On these drives, he was often accompanied by Scott's niece, Rebecca Stewart. Although they were about the same age, Carnegie would later claim that at the time he regarded her as "an elder sister" (Carnegie, 1920, p. 90).

In the early 1870s, while courting Anne Dike Riddle in Pittsburgh, he introduced her to Tom Scott. She and Scott were soon engaged to be married, with Carnegie out of the picture, although there is no evidence that this created a breach between the two men (Wall, 1970, pp. 297–305). What friction existed was apparently confined to their financial relations. Those relations took a decided turn for the worse because of a disastrous investment in the Texas and Pacific Railroad by Scott. Carnegie's unwillingness to bail Scott out during the Panic of 1873 drove a wedge between them, although they continued to do business deals until Scott's death (Nasaw, 2006, p. 155).

After the move to New York in 1867, Carnegie continued socializing with young women as he had in Pittsburgh, even acquiring a reputation as a "ladies man" (Nasaw, 2006, p. 158). One of his pleasures was riding in Central Park, often accompanied by women who also liked to ride. It was in 1880 that he began riding with Louise Whitfield, the daughter of a local merchant and long-time acquaintance of Carnegie's who had died two years before. Although she was almost twenty-two years younger than Andrew, she would become his wife five months after the death of his mother. Romance blossomed early on in their relationship, but it was a difficult courtship.

Louise Whitfield was from a well-to-do family; however, Carnegie was very much richer and, of course, very much older. According to Carnegie, she was indifferent to his attentions at first, and only his illness in the fall of 1886 awakened in her a real interest (Carnegie, 1920, pp. 214–15). The truth of the matter is a bit different. According to Wall (1970, pp. 402–14), the romance began to blossom in 1881 and went through many ups and downs, including a secret engagement in 1883, followed by their breaking it off in the spring of 1884, and a renewal a few months later. Problems in their relationship were exacerbated by his mother's almost total opposition and constant efforts to undermine it. Despite this, they grew closer and closer over the next two years until their marriage on April 22, 1887. From that day, Louise would be the helpmate and love of his life until Carnegie's death in 1919.

Following a honeymoon on the Isle of Wight, the newlyweds spent the summer in a rented country home near Perth. For the next ten years, summers would be spent in Scotland in rented great homes and castles until the Carnegies decided to build their own. When built, Skibo became their permanent summer residence in the northern Highlands. They would entertain extensively, and Louise would be the consummate hostess and overseer.

Chapter Six

Labor Relations

Andrew Carnegie began his working life as an unskilled laborer; however, his intelligence, ambition, initiative, and consistent hard work soon took him out of the cotton mill and the bobbin factory into the position of skilled telegraph operator. Just as Tom Scott of the Pennsylvania Railroad had recognized the talent and ambition in young Andy, so the mature Andrew Carnegie was always alert to the same qualities in his employees and associates. Those who lived up to his expectations were promoted and welcomed into partnerships, while those who did not were not. As he informed students in a speech at Curry Commercial College on June 23, 1885, "The rising man must do something exceptional, and beyond the range of his special department—he must attract attention" (Carnegie, 1885, p. 46). Of course, Carnegie was also ruthless in forcing out those partners who fell short of his expectations.

But what of those employees who were not rising men? What of those who were not particularly intelligent, or not very ambitious, or who exhibited neither quality? What of those employees whose basic purpose is to secure stable employment at good wages and just do their jobs competently for all their working lives? In his autobiography, Carnegie characterizes the capitalist, the employer, and the laborer as legs on a three-legged stool, "all equally indispensable" (Carnegie, 1920, p. 235). Further, he says, "Judging only from the economical results, I believe that higher wages to men who respect their employers and are happy and contented are a good investment, yielding, indeed, big dividends" (Carnegie, 1920, p. 229). The employer, he points out, is relatively insulated against downturns in business conditions so far as their effect on his personal life, whereas the employee is relatively helpless and will suffer privation (Carnegie, 1920, pp. 252–53). Employers should recognize this obvious fact, he says, and all their workmen should expect "appreciation, kind treatment, a fair deal."

In an 1886 *Forum* magazine article on "The Labor Question," Carnegie cast himself as an advocate for negotiation among equals in the event of differences existing between employer and workers—that is, a labor dispute. Through such negotiation, the laborer "rises to the dignity of an independent contractor" (Carnegie, 1886a, p. 93). Of course, Carnegie goes on to say, "The right of the workingmen to combine and to form trades-unions is no less sacred than the right of the manufacturer to enter into associations and conferences with his fellows, and it must sooner or later be conceded" (Carnegie, 1886a, p. 96). Indeed, he says that, in his experience, trades unions are beneficial to both labor and capital—if they are led by intelligent and able men. In his opinion, only ignorant workmen regard capital as the enemy of labor.

Carnegie then suggests four rules to guide the relations between capital and labor: (1) wages should be based on a sliding scale in proportion to output prices and should vary with them; (2) unions should be structured so that "the natural leaders, the best men," rise to the top of those organizations; (3) arbitration of differences should always be peaceful; and (4) no strikes or lockouts should occur during arbitration. As a result of adherence to these principles, he concludes that prosperity and adversity will be shared by capital and labor, and business operations will never be interrupted by internal strife (Carnegie, 1886a, pp. 100–101).

The Haymarket Square riot in Chicago that same year stimulated a second *Forum* article in which Carnegie minimized the importance of labor disputes in general, blaming management and "foreign anarchists" for the few that had occurred. He explicitly condemned the use of strikebreakers, for "there is an unwritten law among the best workmen: 'Thou shalt not take thy neighbor's job'" (Carnegie, 1886b, p. 112). Only for vital services, or as a last resort, should new men take the place of old, wrote Andrew Carnegie in 1886. These words were to prove a source of great discomfort for him in the future, since certain of his past and future actions had not and would not reflect them.

In fact, a comparison of Carnegie's historical actions with his published thoughts on labor relations provides more contrast than congruence. It may be recalled that one of his first actions as Tom Scott's twenty-year-old assistant in the Altoona, Pennsylvania, PRR works was to secure for Scott a list of workers supporting a strike, all of whom Scott immediately fired. In all fairness to Carnegie, this might be considered a case of a young man overeager to please and underestimating the consequences of his actions. A brief summary of other incidents leading up to the tragedy that occurred at the Homestead mill in 1892 will help to clarify matters, if some general judgment is to be reached on Carnegie's words versus his deeds.

In 1865, Kloman and Phipps had merged with the Cyclops Iron Company to form the Union Iron Mills. Although he would not be the majority partner until three years later, when Tom Miller would be forced out and the firm renamed Carnegie, Kloman & Company, Andrew Carnegie was a principal in the formation of the Union Iron Mills and would be included in major decision making. In the summer of 1867 the Pittsburgh area iron puddlers' union, the Sons of Vulcan, struck in opposition to a wage cut. The response by Pittsburgh iron companies, including the Union Mills, was to bring in European workers to replace the strikers. There is no evidence that Carnegie opposed this action for his mill. Indeed, it provided the opportunity for Andrew Kloman to import and hire skilled German metalworkers (Wall, 1970, p. 268).

After Union Mills became Carnegie, Kloman & Company, a prolonged decline in prices and profits of iron manufacturers from 1873 to 1875 led to a proposal by Pittsburgh-area ironmasters to adjust the sliding scale of wages downward, which was again opposed by the Sons of Vulcan. The manufacturers, including Carnegie, Kloman & Company, locked out the puddlers for several months until the loss of business forced them to accede to the union's demands.[1] Again, there is no indication that Carnegie opposed the lockout, as he might have been expected to, given his often-expressed desire to keep his mills open and workforce intact—even at the cost of low profit margins on orders (Nasaw, 2006, pp. 162–63, 174).[2]

So far as Andrew Carnegie's basic attitude toward unions as expressed in his actions is concerned, the Edgar Thomson works opened in 1875 as a nonunion plant. Because it was a Bessemer process works, it needed no puddlers and the skilled labor that was most important was mainly engineering, metallurgical chemistry, and supervisory. More to the point, after the E.T. shut down for several weeks in the fall of 1876 for repairs and refurbishment, Captain Jones announced that all returning workers would be required to sign a no-union pledge. Those who did not sign were not rehired (Nasaw, 2006, pp. 179–80).

During the late 1870s, Carnegie was constantly looking for ways to reduce his production costs. This included introducing incentives for increased productivity by means of production contests and prizes, as well as replacing men with machines, and lobbying Captain Jones to cut wages. Jones always resisted the last mentioned action and successfully argued, "Low wages does not always imply cheap labor" (Nasaw, 2006, p. 182). Jones also argued successfully for changing from twelve- to eight-hour shifts at the E.T. to increase the productivity of the plant's workforce—an experiment that lasted until early 1888 (Wall, 1970, p. 520).[3]

By the spring of 1882, Carnegie's views on unions must have become more favorable. The Amalgamated Association of Iron and Steel Workers, which included the Sons of Vulcan, had successfully organized the craft workers at the Pittsburg Bessemer Steel Company at Homestead. The union leaders then organized a lodge at the E.T. works, and Carnegie persuaded Captain Jones to recognize it. Further, when the Pittsburgh puddlers demanded higher wages, Carnegie, Kloman & Company was the only iron-rolling mill of the thirty-six iron-rolling mills in the Pittsburgh area that agreed to pay them. Carnegie's reputation among workers was so enhanced by this action that he was able to convince the workers at E.T. to accept a wage reduction when steel rail prices were adversely affected by the recession later that year. Steel rail prices continued to decline in 1883, and Carnegie sought and was able to make another wage reduction, both at the E.T. works and at Homestead, which was by then owned by Carnegie Brothers (Nasaw, 2006, pp. 214–15, 248–50).

A violent labor action occurred in July 1884 at the Hartman Steel Works at Beaver Falls, a minor Carnegie investment northwest of Pittsburgh that produced nails and wire rods. Carnegie had bought the company the previous year. The Amalgamated Association of Iron and Steel Workers called a strike. Carnegie had misgivings but supported H. W. Hartman, the company's chairman, in fighting the strike. He imported replacement workers, which led to a riot by strikers, who were subsequently arrested, tried, and convicted and the power of the union broken (Bridge, 1903, pp. 185–86).

Although shifts of eight hours had existed at the E.T. plant since Captain Jones became the manager in the mid-1870s, rail price declines led to the decision to return to the twelve-hour shift practice in the fall of 1884. Jones closed down the plant for maintenance, and when it reopened in February 1885, he rehired only those men willing to work the twelve-hour shift. Improved conditions in late 1885 led to a 10 percent wage increase and labor agitation for the return of the eight-hour shift. Blast furnace employees struck; Jones replaced them with new hires and then shut down the plant when workers in other departments refused to work with them. The reopening of the plant in April 1886 under an eight-hour shift policy was finally forced on Carnegie by the accumulation of unfilled orders from the then-booming demand for steel and resulting higher steel prices (Nasaw, 2006, pp. 259–62).

By the spring of 1886, Carnegie's Carnegie Brothers was the largest investor in the H. C. Frick Coke Company, and Frick's coke workers threatened a strike. Frick favored a lockout if the strike should occur, but Carnegie had steel orders to fill and forced Frick to agree to the coke workers' wage demands (Nasaw, 2006, pp. 289–90). A year later, in the spring of 1887, Connellsville coke workers again called a strike and demanded another wage increase. Again, Frick was prepared to unite with other coke producers and hire replacement workers to break the strike. And again, Carnegie's concern that steel production in both his companies depended on Frick's continued coke production caused him to force Frick to grant the wage increases.[4] This time Frick responded by resigning the presidency of his own company in a sharply worded letter to superintendents Henry Phipps at Braddock and John Walker at Homestead. He accused both Carnegie Brothers and Carnegie, Phipps & Company of prostituting his company's interests to promote their own.[5] It took six months of courting by Carnegie to entice Frick back into the presidency of Frick Coke (Wall, 1970, pp. 494–96).

Carnegie's problems with unions would soon enter a new phase that would result in actions that he would regret for the rest of his life. In December 1887, just before the expiration of the current labor contracts at the E.T. works at Braddock, Carnegie had Captain Jones inform the workforce that when the plant reopened in January 1888, shifts would be twelve hours in length. Both the skilled members of the Knights of Labor and the unskilled nonunion workers struck, and Carnegie instituted a lockout. A few weeks later he offered the striking workers a choice between continuing the eight-hour shift model at lower wages and changing to twelve-hour shifts with a sliding scale of wages. This would allow wages to move in tandem with steel prices, with a guaranteed minimum-wage limit when prices fell. It also would mean the loss of hundreds of jobs at the plant. Lastly, the contract would be for three years to give the sliding scale "a fair trial."

Arbitration dragged on into mid-April, at which point Captain Jones announced that the plant would reopen on April 22 with newly hired labor if necessary. Also, a force of Pinkerton Detective Agency employees arrived at the plant to guard it and those replacement workers when it reopened. A week later, both union and nonunion striking workers began to return to the plant and sign the new labor agreement. The Knights of Labor then called off the strike. E.T. would remain a nonunion plant from then on (Nasaw, 2006, pp. 315–26; Wall, 1970, pp. 527–28). In praise of this new wage arrangement that he had earlier advocated in his 1886 *Forum* article, Carnegie said later, "Of all my services rendered to labor the introduction of the sliding scale is chief. It is the solution of the capital and labor problem, because it really makes them partners—alike in prosperity and adversity" (Carnegie, 1920, p. 247).[6]

Carnegie's success in breaking the union at the E.T. works and introducing the sliding scale brought a period of relative calm to production at Braddock, but his attempt to introduce the same pay plan a year later at his Homestead plant brought another storm and a different result. It began with a managerial announcement on May 18, 1889, that July 1 contract-renewal terms would include a sliding scale of wages linked to output prices and twelve-hour shifts, and these new contracts would be signed by individual workers as a condition of reemployment.[7] There were thirty-eight hundred workers at Homestead, eight hundred of whom were skilled workers represented by the Amalgamated Association of Iron and Steel Workers, others represented by the Knights of Labor, and the rest nonunion. In effect, under the new contracts the unions would no longer be bargaining units. Not surprisingly, they opposed the new arrangement and voted to reject it. The nonunion workers agreed with that decision and also struck.

Expecting Carnegie to hire replacement workers and Pinkerton agents to guard them, the steel workers at Homestead decided to act just as they had in 1882 when they were locked out by Pittsburg Bessemer: they took over the town and prepared to repel any men sent as replacement workers to work the mill. An advisory committee was created "of men chosen from each AAISW lodge [and] armed steelworkers guarded all approaches to the town, allowing no one to enter unless proof was furnished that he was not a black sheep" (Krause, 1992, p. 247).[8]

Homestead was part of Carnegie, Phipps & Company, the board chairman being William A. Abbott, while Frick was chairman at Carnegie Brothers. With Carnegie's express agreement, Abbott had shut down the plant on June 30 and advertised for replacement workers. On July 10, the county sheriff arrived in Homestead on a train escorting thirty-one black, Italian, and Eastern European replacement workers. They were met by a barrier of two thousand Homesteaders, who drove off most of the new workers under a hail of stones and then forced three of them, and the hiring agent, to proceed down a mile-long gauntlet of beatings. On July 12, the sheriff and 125 deputies returned, only to be met by a larger crowd, which so cowed them that the deputies dropped their revolvers, threw off their badges and coats, and retreated to Pittsburgh (Krause, 1992, pp. 247–48).

The workers at the E.T. plant then threatened a sympathy strike. To Carnegie's dismay, Abbott caved in the face of this double threat of violence and strikes at both plants. The result was that three-year sliding scale contracts were signed at Homestead, with the Amalgamated union becoming the exclusive representative of the workforce.[9] Carnegie admonished Abbott for failing to continue a lockout that he expected would have produced the same results as those at E.T. Nevertheless, the twelve-hour shift with a sliding scale of wages now existed at both plants and the Homestead workers were under contract until June 30, 1892 (Wall, 1970, pp. 528–30; Nasaw, 2006, pp. 368–71).

While production resumed at Homestead in the summer of 1889, the three-year labor contract with the workforce at the E.T. plant that had been signed in 1888 would become the next point of contention. It was to expire on December 31, 1890. The death of Captain Jones a year earlier as a result of a blast furnace accident was a tragedy for both Carnegie and Braddock. The loss of the superintendent who had the best relationship with an important part of Carnegie's total workforce would change the context of future labor contract negotiations—and not for the better.

Carnegie wanted the new three-year contract to continue the existing wage rates and twelve-hour shifts, while workers at the E.T. plant wanted a return to the eight-hour shift arrangement that had existed for so long under Jones's superintendency. Carnegie was intransigent on both points and prepared to replace any worker who struck. When a mob of unskilled workers managed to shut down a part of the plant on January 1, Frick and Charles Schwab—the plant superintendent—armed some workers with rifles, pistols, and clubs. With the local sheriff's approval, these "deputies" were prepared to repel any future assault. None came, and the E.T. plant was soon in operation under the contract that Carnegie had wanted (Nasaw, 2006, pp. 385–90).

A little more than a year afterward, there was another strike in the Connellsville region against the Frick coke works. Frick and Carnegie not only refused to concede to the strikers but also posted new wage rates and were prepared to hire whatever replacements were necessary to continue coke production. Some of the strikers subsequently attacked the coke works and were repelled by private police and sheriff's deputies brought in by Frick. Seven workers were killed and others injured in the confrontation (Warren, 1996, p. 169).

Carnegie not only supported Frick's actions but also suggested that intervention by the state militia be requested. After another violent confrontation, the governor did send in the state militia to restore order. Then Frick hired one hundred Pinkerton agents, who were deputized by the local sheriff to protect replacement workers and the nonstriking men in his workforce. The strike was finally called off on May 27 (Nasaw, 2006, pp. 390–93). Because of the mob violence and deaths, it had been the most serious of the labor disputes faced by Carnegie up to this point. A year later, worse was to come at Homestead. Steel workers and others would join together in mob actions that constituted a general assault on the rule of law, property rights, and freedom of association.

Carnegie Steel Company, Ltd., was incorporated July 1, 1892, at a capitalization of $25 million. It represented the formal merger of Carnegie, Phipps & Company and Carnegie Brothers. Andrew Carnegie held a 55.33 percent ownership share, Henry Clay Frick and Henry Phipps 11 percent each, Carnegie's cousin George "Dod" Lauder 4 percent, and the other nineteen partners 2 percent or less each, with 3.67 percent held in trust for the admission of future partners. Carnegie and Phipps retired from active management, and Henry Clay Frick became chairman of the board and chief executive officer of the new corporation (Harvey, 1928, pp. 103–5).

The birth of Carnegie Steel coincided with a lockout and strike at the Homestead works that led to a violent struggle and mob action that caused the deaths of three Pinkerton National Detective Agency guards and seven Homestead steel workers. The tragic events of early July 1892 included the wounding of hundreds of Pinkertons as well as many members of the attacking mob. After the battle at the plant and subsequent occupation of the town by 8,500 Pennsylvania National Guardsmen, there were 133 indictments for riot, conspiracy, treason, and murder brought against ninety-three steel workers, none of whom were subsequently convicted (Krause, 1992, pp. 409–10, fn. 2 and 4). It was also the end of unionization at Homestead—the very end that the initial company lockout was intended to accomplish and the union response of a strike meant to prevent. The following is a brief outline of the lockout, strike, and subsequent violence—the calamity now known as "the Homestead Strike."

In July 1891, William Martin, a former secretary for the Amalgamated Association of Iron and Steel Workers, was employed by Carnegie as the head of his labor department. Martin was set to work drawing up the sliding scale of wages proposal that was to be presented to the workers at the Homestead plant in the spring of 1892. Current employment contracts would expire on June 30 of that year, and Carnegie wanted new contracts that would reduce production costs.

As Martin surveyed wage rates at other mills in the Pittsburgh area, he found that Carnegie was paying skilled workers at Homestead 50 percent more than his competitors, as well as paying his other workers above-market wages, even at his nonunion mills at Braddock and Duquesne (Krause, 1992, p. 291). To the managerial problems posed by union control of working conditions at the Homestead plant since the settling of the 1889 strike, this information added a second reason for Carnegie and Frick to want to eliminate the Amalgamated union's hold over their workforce.

In the spring of 1892, Carnegie and Frick decided that the expiration of the current labor contracts at Homestead would be the end of the control of the plant by the Amalgamated Association; after July 1, the plant was to be a nonunion plant, as were the plants at Duquesne and Braddock. Only eight hundred of the thirty-eight hundred men employed in the Homestead plant were members of the Amalgamated union; yet that union of skilled craftsmen—in cooperation with the Knights of Labor and the nonunion part of the workforce—effectively represented the entire plant workforce. This had to end if managerial control was to be reestablished and lower production costs attained.

Although corporate profits in 1891 had been $4.3 million, prices of steel billets produced at the plant had fallen from $27 to $22 a ton, while the current sliding-scale minimum that was based on the billet price remained at $25 a ton.[10] On April 4, 1892, before his departure for his annual six-month residency in Scotland, Carnegie sent to Frick a draft of a notice to all Homestead employees that the next contract would be a nonunion one. He also directed that the plant stockpile billets against the possibility of a strike. The plant was producing armor plate under a lucrative Department of the Navy contract, and Carnegie wanted no interruption in delivery in the event that a strike was called through the rejection of the new contract terms by the steel workers. If there was a strike, Carnegie told Frick to close the plant and lock out the workers until agreement was reached (Wall, 1970, pp. 541–42).

Instead of posting the notice, Frick began negotiating with representatives of the union. He wanted three key concessions: a reduction of the scale minimum to $22 a ton for workers paid by tonnage of billets produced, wage cuts in departments that had the most increased productivity because of new machinery, and a change in the contract expiration date from June 30 to December 31, with an initial contract for eighteen months. The union was given until June 24 to accept these terms. After that date, union representatives were told that the firm would only deal with individual steel workers (Bridge, 1903, p. 207).

Frick claimed that the December 31 date would be more convenient for both parties since business was slow at that time of year, and workers and the company could better tolerate a stoppage if one were to occur. Also, materials contracts were typically made at the beginning of the year, at which time the company had to estimate the wages it would be able to pay.[11] The union's view was that the proposed tonnage rates were too low, and living expenses were higher in winter, making contract negotiations too favorable for Carnegie Steel at that time. Also, greater general unemployment in midwinter would make it easier for the firm to hire replacement workers in the event of a strike or lockout. The union consequently opposed the new contract terms (Krause, 1992, pp. 303–5).

Meanwhile, Frick had an eleven-foot-high, three-mile-long wooden fence constructed around the perimeter of the plant property. It was whitewashed and topped with three strands of barbed wire that added another eighteen inches to its height. Holes cut in it periodically appeared to be gun ports. There were twelve-foot-high towers topped with electric searchlights built at the ends of the tallest plant buildings to illuminate the mill yard at night. Water cannons were placed at each plant entrance. Frick also made an arrangement in June with the Pinkerton National Detective Agency to supply three hundred of its guards for the first week in July. It was obvious that he expected mob action at some point and was preparing for it. Given his experience with the recent strikes and violence at the Frick coke works, and his knowledge of the past actions at Homestead by the Amalgamated Association in 1882 and 1889, this was not an unreasonable assumption for him to make. Nonetheless, these actions were provocative and suggested that he had no expectation of reaching an agreement on the new contracts with the steel workers.[12] The workers themselves believed that Frick intended to force a bloody conflict with the union (Burgoyne, 1893, pp. 21–22).

No agreement having been reached between the company and the union, on June 28 Frick shut down the armor plate mill and the open-hearth department.[13] Completion of the shutdown of the entire plant the next day, one day before expiration of the current contracts with workers, made this a lockout of workers by the company. In response, effigies of Frick and plant superintendent John A. Potter were hung on telegraph poles that night. On July 1, all workers walked out of the plant in a general strike responding to the lockout. This walkout occurred despite the fact that one thousand of the mechanics had signed a new wage agreement on June 20 with Carnegie Steel (Demarest, 1992, p. 35).

Rumors circulated in the town that an army of Pinkerton guards would soon arrive, escorting replacement workers. Members of the Amalgamated Association met and appointed an advisory committee, selected from their eight lodges and chaired by a roller named Hugh C. O'Donnell. Its job was to organize patrols to keep the peace in the town and to station pickets to alert workers of any approaching Pinkertons escorting replacement workers.[14] The burgess (mayor) of the town, John McLuckie, also a plant employee, ordered all saloons closed. The steam launch *Edna* and a flotilla of boats of various types were soon patrolling the river in the vicinity of the plant.

On July 2, all Homestead plant steel workers were paid off and discharged. Frick notified county sheriff William H. McCleary that Pinkertons escorting replacement workers would soon be coming up the river from Pittsburgh and requested that they all be deputized. Frick later testified before a congressional investigating committee that McCleary agreed, while McCleary denied this claim. On the morning of July 5, Frick informed the sheriff that men were preventing access to the company's property and threatening to damage it. He requested protection. In response, the sheriff and several of his deputies went to Homestead, and McCleary informed a large crowd of steel workers that the company had the right to bring in men and operate the plant. He was told that this would not be allowed to happen, and he and his deputies were escorted to the river, which they crossed, and then went by rail back to Pittsburgh. Effectively, the steel workers of the Homestead plant had taken over the town and were in defiance of the law and the legal authority attempting to enforce it.

Another attempt to enforce the rule of law in Homestead was made in the late afternoon by Sheriff McCleary. He sent Deputy Sheriff Samuel H. Cluley and ten other deputies by rail to Homestead to post a proclamation at various sites in the town. The proclamation notified anyone preventing access to the plant or threatening violence to its employees or property that those acts were unlawful, and anyone committing them was subject to be arrested and prosecuted. A crowd of striking steel workers surrounded the deputies, and they were soon marched to the river, forced to board the steamer *Edna*, and taken to Glenwood village to ride by rail back to Pittsburgh (Demarest, 1992, pp. 68–69).

The evening of July 5 found three hundred Pinkerton agents, led by Captain F. H. Heinde, at the Davis Island dam on the Ohio River, just north of the confluence of the Allegheny and Monongahela rivers in Pittsburgh. Along with the county sheriff's chief deputy, Colonel Joseph N. Gray, they boarded two 125-by-20-foot barges after midnight to be towed by the tugs *Little Bill* and *Tide* to the Homestead plant landing. The *Tide* soon broke down, and the *Little Bill* now took both barges in tow. Also on board with the Pinkerton agents were cooks and waiters, as well as Pinkerton uniforms, 300 pistols, 250 Winchester rifles, and ammunition for the weapons. One of the union advisory committee pickets spotted the boats and barges in Pittsburgh and telegraphed the news to Amalgamated Association headquarters at 2:30 a.m. on July 6.

As dawn was breaking, the tug and the barges neared the plant to find thousands of steel workers and their families gathered on both shores of the Monongahela. Shots were fired at the barges and the tug, and a large crowd broke down a section of the company fence protecting the mill's private wharf and stood waiting for any attempt by the men on the barges to land on the company's property.[15] When the gangplank was run from the barge to the landing, Captain Heinde and two other Pinkerton agents confronted the men gathered at its end and attempted to step ashore. Heinde was clubbed and then shot, more shots rang out from the crowd, and the Pinkertons on the barges replied with rifle fire.[16] The initial battle lasted ten minutes. Two Pinkerton agents and two steel workers were killed, and many others on both sides suffered gunshot wounds.

The mob violence that followed was horrific. Workers piled steel beams on the banks that sloped up from the river to fortify them, and snipers, using their own weapons and weapons distributed at union headquarters, sporadically fired at the barges. The tug sailed away with the agents wounded in the initial battle, marooning the two barges full of Pinkerton guards under fire at the wharf. There was a second battle at 10 a.m., and thousands of people gathered on the hills above the town and mill to watch. Two twenty-pound cannons were used ineffectually by the workers to fire at the barges from the shore. One of the cannon shots actually decapitated a steel worker. The tug returned at 11 a.m. to attempt a rescue of the barges, but it was riddled with bullets and driven off downstream with one crewman killed.

Serious attempts by the steel workers and other members of the amassed onshore mob to massacre all the men on the barges occurred throughout the day. Burning rafts were sent on the river in an attempt to set the barges on fire but missed their targets. Dynamite was thrown onto the barges, but it either went out or exploded, causing minimal damage. Oil was pumped onto the surface of the water and set on fire, but it floated away. A railroad car loaded with oil and wood was set on fire and rolled down the steep bank toward the barges but stopped short. Natural gas was poured on the barges and rockets shot at it, but the gas failed to ignite. Flags of truce, put up by the Pinkertons, were shot down by the rioting workers.

Meanwhile, armed reinforcements of workers from the E.T. mill at Braddock, and from Pittsburgh, flowed into the town, and the mob swelled by the thousands. Journalists flocked into Homestead from Pittsburgh, New York, Chicago, Philadelphia, Cleveland, and Baltimore, mingling with the workers during the battle. Sheriff McCleary telegraphed appeals for National Guard intervention to Governor Robert E. Pattison at 10 a.m., noon, and 2 p.m., to no avail. He was told that quelling the violence was his responsibility; however, he was unable to deputize a sufficient number of men to counter the thousands in the mob. Mobilization of the Pennsylvania National Guard would not be ordered by Governor Pattison until July 10, and then only after one of his envoys had been kidnapped and driven from the town.

In late afternoon of July 6, William Weihe, current national president of the Amalgamated Association, along with other national officers, arrived from Pittsburgh and pleaded with the mob to cease firing and to allow the Pinkertons to surrender and leave. At 5 p.m. the Pinkertons put up a white flag; after a parley on the gangplank, it was agreed that the men on the barges would be allowed to surrender and be escorted safely to the town opera house as prisoners. A gauntlet of two lines of workers and their families and other mob members six hundred yards long formed, and members of it then beat, clubbed, stoned, stabbed, robbed, and tore off the clothes of the agents as they were marched through the plant and town streets. More than 140 of the 300 Pinkerton guards were wounded, and 30 of them went to a hall used as a makeshift hospital with broken arms, gouged eyes, head wounds, and other injuries.[17] The rest were taken by the sheriff on a train to Pittsburgh at midnight, to be sent to the east on the PRR at 10 a.m. in the morning. Meanwhile, the mob in Homestead looted the barges of their contents (including the weapons), set the barges on fire, and left them as smoking hulks.

In the aftermath of the battle and departure of the Pinkerton agents, Homestead remained under the control of the workers for several days, and they continued to repulse efforts by the sheriff to assert his legal authority. Finally, in the face of Sheriff McCleary's inability to reassert the rule of law in Homestead, a July 10 request from him to Governor Robert E. Pattison led the governor to order Major General George R. Snowden to mobilize the eighty-five hundred members of the Pennsylvania National Guard.[18] The troops arrived in Homestead on the morning of July 12 and quickly occupied the town and the surrounding high ground. They would remain to guard the plant and police the town until October 13. With the town now under martial law, the plant reopened with replacement workers, and the struggle between the unemployed steel workers and Carnegie Steel entered a new phase.

In sympathy with the Homestead strikers, strikes were called at Union Mills on July 15, at Beaver Falls the next day, and at the Duquesne plant on July 23. On that same day, the Lithuanian anarchist Alexander Berkman, a political associate and lover of anarcho-communist agitator Emma Goldman, shot and stabbed Henry Clay Frick in an assault at Frick's Pittsburgh office. Before this incident, unions all over the country and in the United Kingdom had issued statements and passed resolutions supporting the strikers and condemning Carnegie and Frick. Although Berkman had no connection with the striking workers and Frick made a full recovery, outside support and sympathy for the strikers began to recede after Berkman's murderous attack.

Frick had earlier imposed a deadline of July 21 for striking workers to return to their jobs, and many did, but the majority remained on strike until declining strike funds and the onset of winter brought an official end to the strike. On November 21, the Amalgamated Association finally declared the mill open. Although no strikers were convicted of any of the charges brought against them, including murder, riot, conspiracy, and insurrection, at least twenty-five hundred of the thirty-eight hundred striking workers never found employment in the Homestead mill again. Their leaders, including McDonnell and McLuckie, were blacklisted from any steel industry jobs for life.

From mid-July until the end of the strike in November, there were periodic assaults on replacement workers and attempts to prevent the mill's operation. On October 6, a bomb was thrown into a hotel that housed replacement workers and blew a hole in the floor of the dining room, but there were no casualties. By the end of October, the sheriff had almost two hundred deputies employed in trying to prevent violent acts by the strikers. One particularly bizarre event was the attempted arsenic poisoning of the plant's workers by cooks in league with the Pittsburgh district leader of the Knights of Labor. After trial and conviction in early 1893, he was sentenced to seven years in prison while three cooks got seven, five, and three years, respectively.

In his autobiography, Andrew Carnegie (1920, pp. 231–32) claims that, if it had been his decision, he never would have brought in guards and attempted to keep the plant open, as did his partners. Instead, he would have shut the plant until the union accepted the firm's offer. He adds, "Nothing I have ever had to meet in all my life, before or since, wounded me so deeply. No pangs remain of any wound received in my business career save that of Homestead."

Unfortunately for these later expressions of intention and remorse, his words and actions at the time of the lockout and strike do not support them. As previously mentioned, Carnegie was in full accord with Frick's plan to reopen the plant as a nonunion one, and he supported Frick's intransigence in the negotiations with union representatives. He even wrote Frick from England on May 4 offering his unqualified support for any actions Frick might take in the coming confrontation (Wall, 1970, p. 545) and twice sent letters of support in June (Bridge, 1903, pp. 205–6). It was also in June that he took actions to provide sources of replacement workers should the plant close and the union fail to agree to the new contract terms.

Carnegie's support for Frick's actions at the time is also shown by the fact that, the day after the battle, he sent Frick a telegram that said in part, "All anxiety gone since you stand firm. Never employ one of these rioters. Let grass grow over works" (Wall, 1970, p. 565). Even worse for Carnegie's credibility, in March of the next year Carnegie wrote Whitelaw Reid, editor and publisher of the New York *Tribune* and the Republican vice presidential nominee in the coming election, denying that he had had any idea that replacement workers had been used to reopen the Homestead plant (Wall, 1970, p. 568). Reid had corresponded with Carnegie in a vain attempt to intercede on behalf of the Amalgamated Association the previous July, while Frick had specifically informed Carnegie of his plan to deliver replacement workers at the time (Nasaw, 2006, p. 419).

Henry Clay Frick's conduct during this period stands in stark contrast to that of Carnegie. Frick placed the company's contract requirements before representatives of the Amalgamated Association, giving a June 24 deadline, after which the company would deal only with individual workers. He may have expected a refusal, since he and Carnegie had agreed that the company would be operated the same as the nonunion plants at Duquesne and Braddock after July 1, but he did exactly as he said he would. He shut down the plant and locked out the workers at the end of June after the June 24 deadline passed without an agreement having been reached. He also prepared the plant for possible mob activity in the event that he had to (as indeed he did) bring in replacement workers to operate the plant and protect them and the company's property.

When the workers struck, he presented another deadline of July 21 for individual applications and hired many of those who applied and who had not taken part in the riot and violence against the Pinkerton guards and the company's property. During the occupation of the town by forces organized by the workers' advisory committee, he informed the county sheriff of his planned employment of Pinkerton guards to protect the plant and any workers hired to replace those on strike and requested the deputizing of those guards and protection for his plant and employees by the local authorities. He also kept Carnegie informed of the ongoing situation as it developed.

After the arrival of National Guard troops and the occupation of the town by them, Frick reopened the plant and called for legal action against the rioters. During this whole period, he refused every request to bargain with representatives of the union that had stimulated the mob action and occupied and destroyed the company's property. He was a man of remarkable consistency and unswerving determination, and he got what he wanted—a lower-cost, nonunion plant at Homestead. By 1897, plant production had increased by 28 percent with a workforce 25 percent smaller. In 1901, when Carnegie Steel would be sold to J. P. Morgan to become part of U.S. Steel, the Homestead mill was the largest steel mill in the world and one of the most efficient (Warren, 1996, pp. 101, 109).

Whether the beneficial results of the lockout and strike for the Carnegie Steel Company, Ltd., were worth what it cost in lives, injuries, thievery, and destruction of property at Homestead is impossible to assess. One question that can be resolved is whether the Homestead workers' belief that they were acting in defense of their jobs, in which they had property rights, has any grounding in economic or political theory. Wall (1970, p. 581) expresses this understanding in general terms as the mill workers' belief "that they had acquired a proprietary interest in the mill, for if it possessed their minds and bodies most of their working hours, then surely they also possessed it." Nasaw (2006, p. 415) is more direct: "The Homestead workers, especially the skilled ones, had an ownership stake in the mills. . . . They regarded their right to remain at their jobs as sacrosanct [and] would not give up their positions without a fight." Speaking to a reporter for the *New York World* on July 3, town burgess John McLuckie said, "We are asking nothing but our rights, and we will have them if it requires force to get them" (Nasaw, 2006, p. 418).

Krause characterizes the Homestead of 1892 as "the nation's preeminent labor town" (1992, p. 253) and the Homestead conflict that year as one "between the pursuit of private interest and the defense of the common good" (1992, p. 6). He claims that the conflict was actually "about the right of individuals [Carnegie et al.] to accumulate unlimited wealth and privilege versus the right of individuals [Carnegie Steel employees] to enjoy security in their jobs and dignity in their homes." The battle itself was one "over conflicting property rights" (Krause, 1992, p. 313). The firm was claiming the right to hire and fire and manage its property as it saw fit, while the steel workers were claiming the right to their jobs and the union that had secured them. In Krause's narrative, the Pinkerton agents were "the approaching enemy," their attempt to land on Carnegie Steel property was "an attack," and the response by the mob on the banks of the Monongahela was "Homestead's defense" (Krause, 1992, p. 16).

In a further discussion about conflicting concepts of property rights, Krause (1992, p. 339) favorably presents the views of James Boyce, an Amalgamated Association leader at the time of the lockout and strike. Boyce said that all the workers had done was to prevent their jobs from being stolen. They owned those jobs. After all, it was they who had built the mill and generated the company's profits. Further, said Boyce, "he and his co-workers had a right to a competence, a sufficiency of the means to live comfortably, and a right to the means to ensure that such a life was indeed possible, that is, a right to a job" (Krause, 1992, p. 343).

Earlier, Krause (1992, p. 120) had quoted a January 8, 1876, editorial in the *National Labor Tribune* that presented the rationale for the Amalgamated Association as "the conviction that there is a certain rate of wages which men should receive for their labor . . . regardless of the empirical and cruel law of supply and demand." This is, as summarized by Krause, "because the calculus of the market ignored the rights of all laborers." The competitive system was unjust, the wage system "unnatural" and creating "wage slaves." The workers at the Homestead mill wondered why prices of steel should determine wages. They asked, "Were not the English steelworkers better off under a system whereby wages determined prices?" (Wall, 1970, p. 554).

In contrast, Carnegie's view that labor costs needed to be cut, as expressed in his March 30, 1889, dedication speech at the workers' library in Braddock, is interpreted by Krause to mean that Carnegie saw "virtually no connection between earnings and output: the labor market and the price of steel, not [labor?] productivity should determine wages" (Krause, 1992, p. 245). This is a puzzling interpretation. What Carnegie said in that speech was that the sliding scale he advocated for all his plants would tie wages to the price of steel. This would create a partnership between employers and employees. The problem that he had with the Amalgamated Association at the Homestead mill, he said, was that the union was forcing him to pay higher wages than his competitors were paying. This was "driving away our trade," presumably by means of his competitors' consequently lower prices (Demarest, 1992, pp. 1–2).

Carnegie did see a connection between earnings and output. He wanted to tie them together by tying wage rates to steel prices and selling more output by becoming more competitive. Regarding the question of what that level of wages should be, he may well have believed that they should be set in the labor market by the interaction between labor supply and labor demand since he and his competitors hired their steel workers from that market. Whether his idea of tying wage rates to steel prices at Carnegie Steel would have conflicted with paying market wage rates is another question. As William Martin had discovered in trying to design a sliding scale, Carnegie's workers were already paid above market rates.

To resolve the problem presented by these conflicting theories of property rights, wages, and the relation between wages and profits, it is necessary to recognize the profound conflict between two opposed theories of economic value and price. These are, respectively, the eighteenth- and nineteenth-century labor theory of value and the late nineteenth-century marginal utility theory of value. The latter permanently replaced the labor theory as an explanation of the relation between prices and wages for all but a few economic theorists, thus revolutionizing both economic theory and its use in the historical explanation of the market process.

In 1690, in chapter 5 of John Locke's *Second Treatise of Government*, he argued that man acquires a property right in anything he has removed from its natural state. This, he wrote, is because man owns himself, his body's labor, and anything with which he mixes his labor. Further, Locke asserted that labor "puts the difference in value on everything," meaning that relative values of things are determined by the relative amounts of labor exerted to obtain them. This was an early and simple way of stating what is known as "the labor theory of value," and it tied the concepts of property rights and relative values to one another theoretically.

Adam Smith refined the labor theory and made it more complex in his justly famous 1776 economic treatise *On the Nature and Causes of the Wealth of Nations*. Smith's treatise assumes the existence of private property rights while he argues for the theory that the exchange values of everything traded are determined by the absolute amounts of labor that are required to produce them. In chapter 5 of book 1, Smith asserts that "labour . . . is the real measure of the exchangeable value of all commodities" and the "real price" of everything. Nevertheless, because the labor exerted to produce different commodities differs in "hardship endured" and "ingenuity exerted," the "higgling and bargaining of the market" adjusts actual market prices for differences in the quality of labor used to produce those commodities. In Smith's chapter 8 on wages, he allows that although labor creates the value of everything produced by man, rent for land used and profits for capital stock advanced must be deducted from the total value produced for all but the completely independent workman.

David Ricardo's *On the Principles of Political Economy and Taxation* (1817) turned Smith's theory of wage and price determination into one of distribution of income and resultant class conflict. Ricardo argued that subsistence wages depend on the price of grain, and the price of grain is set by the application of labor to land in agriculture. As agricultural production extends to less fertile land, more labor is required to produce a given amount of grain, thus raising grain prices and the rent on land. Subsistence wages in agriculture as well as industry would have to rise as a result, which would reduce profits in industry. So, economic development means rising rents and an inverse relation between wages and profits. This creates conflict between capitalists and laborers.

The next step was taken by John Stuart Mill in his 1848 *Principles of Political Economy, with Some of Their Applications to Social Philosophy*. Mill accepted the labor theory of value but argued that production of wealth is governed by natural laws, while the distribution of the output is one of human design and is not necessarily to be ruled by property rights. This meant that labor unions and government could intervene to increase wages, improve working conditions, and change the distribution of the wealth produced by labor.

Lastly, Karl Marx took the labor theory of value of Smith and the class conflict theory of Ricardo and extended them into a theory of the exploitation of labor by capital that would lead to the inevitable collapse of the system he christened "capitalism." According to Marx's three-volume work, *Das Kapital*, the first volume of which was published in 1867 and the other two after his death in 1883, all value is produced by labor and all prices determined by units of "socially necessary" labor time. Values and prices differ among products by the lesser or greater numbers of units of labor time consumed in their respective productions. The exploiting capitalist pays the worker only subsistence wages and expropriates the surplus value that labor produces. The whole system is sustained by the institution of private property rights, which places the worker, who owns only his own labor, at the mercy of the capitalist owners of the means of production. Marx argued that the increasing immiseration of the laboring class—the proletariat—by the capitalists would eventually lead to revolution, the abolishing of the institution of private property, and the classless society.

In light of the eighteenth- and nineteenth-century developments in the labor theories of value and of property rights, it is not difficult to see why workers involved in the late nineteenth-century labor movement—especially those in organized unions—would see themselves as the source of the value and profits produced by the firms for which they worked. During the preceding 150-year period, the source of value, and thus of income and wealth, had been viewed as a supply-side phenomenon by mainstream economic theorists, particularly in the English-speaking world. Their view was that it is labor exerted in a production process that produces value, income, and wealth using raw materials and tools.

For factory workers, especially those in the labor movement, this also would be the obvious view of the production of valuable things. They may not have read the mainstream scholarly and other writers on economic subjects, but intellectual products always trickle down into popular writing and disperse into the general understanding of members of the society at large. Workers could see every working day that they used their labor, aided by tools and machinery, to transform natural resources into products that were sold for their production costs plus a profit. Obviously, the end value—the price—would seem to be merely a summarization of the values expressed in costs and added together during the production process. As the Amalgamated

Association leader James Boyce must have believed, since the men working in the plant produced the goods and the profits, the firm owed its employees a decent living, and their jobs were the security for that. The end goods were the property of the firm, but the jobs were the rightful property of the workers whose valuable labor produced those valuable goods.

In the 1870s, three economists in three different countries published books that revolutionized the theory of the market process—each in a distinctive way. All three used what came to be termed the "principle of diminishing marginal utility" as a central device in their respective explications and thus inaugurated "the Marginal Revolution" in economic theory. William Stanley Jevons (1835–1882) in London, England; Leon Walras (1834–1910) in Lausanne, Switzerland; and Carl Menger (1840–1921) in Vienna, Austria, independently developed, wrote, and published their theories in their respective countries to little initial acclaim or success. Later, their names would become internationally known and celebrated. Jevons and Walras used mathematics to present their theories, and both argued for "equilibria," or states of rest, for their models. Menger viewed the market process as a complex of human activities created by choosing and interacting with individual persons set in real time and having no equilibria; consequently, he used a literary rather than a mathematical method in his theoretical explication. Menger's *Grundsaetze der Volkswirtschaftslehre* (1871), translated into English in 1950 as *Principles of Economics*, is the foundational text for what is now known as "the Austrian School of Economics" and contains the clearest presentation of the new theory of value and its implications for the market process. Menger argues that the source of value and the determination of the values of individual things begin in the evaluation by individual human beings of which means will best meet their ends. Against Mill's view that production is determined by natural law, while distribution is one of human design, Menger argues that the market process includes production, exchange, and distribution—all three of which are governed by definite economic laws. He says,

> Whether and under what conditions a thing is *useful* to me, whether and under what conditions it is a *good*, whether and under what conditions it is an *economic good*, whether and under what conditions it possesses *value* for me and how large the *measure* of this value is for me, whether and under what conditions an *economic exchange* of goods will take place between two economizing individuals, and the limits within which a *price* can be established if an exchange does occur—these and many other matters are fully as independent

of my will as any law of chemistry is of the will of the practicing chemist. (Menger, [1871] 1950, p. 48)

It is also apparent from Menger's words that he had shifted the view of the source of value from a supply-side to a demand-side perspective. Value was the result of an evaluation by a person, not a result of an application of labor. This had revolutionary implications for the theory of production. First, Menger identified a "good" as anything that is believed useful and can be used to satisfy a human need. Goods that can immediately be consumed he termed "first-order goods." Those that can be used to produce first-order goods he termed "second-order goods." Goods used to produce second-order goods were "third order," and so on. Nevertheless, "the order of a good is nothing inherent in the good itself and still less a property of it"; it is dependent on the human purpose in question and how the good is perceived as fitting into a hierarchy that produces a first-order good (Menger, [1871] 1950, p. 58). Bread is a first-order good if it is used by a consumer for sustenance; it is a higher-order good if it is being used in a restaurant or factory to make croutons.

Further, "goods of higher order acquire and maintain their goods character . . . as a result of human foresight" (Menger, [1871] 1950, p. 68). A higher-order good like the palm oil used to make popcorn would lose its goods character if people became convinced that it was unhealthy and quit using it to make popcorn. Labor skilled in palm oil production would lose its value for that purpose also, unless palm oil could be used to produce something else of value.

"Economic goods" are those goods for which human requirements exceed the available quantity—that is, they are scarce. If first-order (consumer) goods are economic goods, then higher-order goods used to make them depend for their economic character on those consumer goods' character. This means that labor, tools, machinery, raw materials are only economic goods if they are scarce and can be used to produce a first-order good that is an economic good—meaning that it is scarce and viewed as valuable.

This theory completely negates the labor theory of value. It implies that the labor that is used to produce valuable consumer goods is only valuable because of its use to do that and because it is scarce. Rather than goods produced by labor obtaining their value from the labor exerted to produce them, the labor exerted to produce them is only valuable because of the value of the goods produced. Only products whose sale is profitable justify employing the labor to produce them.

If "value does not exist outside of the consciousness of men" (Menger, [1871] 1950, p. 121), how does an individual unit of any good obtain its value? Menger's answer was that the value of that unit is equal to the subjective satisfaction that an individual person would expect to forgo if that unit of the good were removed from his possession and control. This idea implied that if an individual possessed a stock of a particular good, and its units were interchangeable in need-satisfying character, any particular unit could be the one lost. Since the lost satisfaction would be from the use that the individual ranked lowest among possible uses of the good, all units of the stock are viewed as having the same low value.

Nevertheless, if the individual's stock was diminished by more than one unit, then, as his stock diminished, he would value each of the remaining units more highly. This is because the subjective satisfactions he would be forced to forgo would be higher up on his scale of ranking than if he had more units and could use them for less important satisfactions. What Menger had deduced was the principle of diminishing marginal utility, although he didn't give it that name. In its modern form, it says that an increasing stock of anything is devoted to uses that diminish in importance as the stock grows, and vice versa. This means that individual units of the stock diminish in value as a person's stock increases. If I have only a cup of water, I will drink it to preserve my life. If I have an assured supply of thousands of gallons of water, I might swim in it, water my lawn with it, and use it to wash my dog.

How does this relate to market prices? Individual persons who are trading with one another always trade away what they value less in return for something they value more. That is the purpose of trading. Menger said that individuals stop trading when no surplus of value can be obtained by trading anymore, or at any higher rate. The market price is just the trading ratio that exists at that point in time as expressed in the medium of exchange—money. The value of objects traded is subjective to the individuals trading; the price is an objective historical fact not quantitatively related to subjective value. Rather than the amount of labor exerted being a determinant of the value of the product produced and helping to set the price, the market determines what is valuable to those producing and trading and sets prices. Labor is valuable if it produces a product that is valuable in the market, and the price of labor itself is also set in markets. It is set through the interaction of those trying to hire labor they believe can be used to produce marketable products at market prices that are profitable and those trying to sell their labor to the highest bidder.

Menger did one more thing in his book that is relevant to our question about the differing views of value at issue in the discussion of the Homestead Strike: he clarified the relations between the theory of value and that of property rights. Rather than a direct tie, as with Locke, who wrote that the exertion of labor created both value and property rights in valuable things, Menger presented an indirect one. He argued that economic goods are by definition valuable and scarce goods, and everyone cannot be equally successful in their production and possession. The institution of private property rights is a social device necessitated by this fact. So, in his view, scarcity is both the basis for the human economy (in which men interact to produce, trade, and consume economic goods) and the basis for "the so-called *protection of ownership*, the basis of property" (Menger, [1871] 1950, p. 97). Property rights are a utilitarian device to prevent social conflict. Menger added the statement that "men are communists whenever possible under existing natural conditions" ([1871] 1950, p. 100), meaning that there is no conflict over things that are not scarce and thus no need for property rights in them.

To apply the foregoing history and theory to the Homestead situation in 1892, it must first be realized that a job is not property. *Job* is a word applied to a related series of human actions that are part of a production process. They are not a static collection, but rather change as the production process changes. A "job" is not a higher-order good, although the labor exerted to perform it can be. The process called a "job" exists because the principals of a firm believe that something of value can be produced by that means that will earn revenue greater than the costs of producing it. It will do so if the good produced is an economic good in the opinion of consumers and they are willing to pay more for it than it will cost the firm to produce. The entrepreneurial job—as Israel Kirzner defines it—is to be alert to the existence of those possible profit opportunities.

In the end, the value and resultant price of the good produced is not the result of the labor exerted to produce it; the value and resultant price of the good is what confers value on the labor needed to produce it, therefore creating the job for the worker who will exert the labor. The price of the labor is determined in markets where individuals and firms demand labor, on the one hand, and supply it, on the other. Demanders wishing to produce valuable goods and suppliers wanting jobs interact to channel what is perceived as valuable labor into the production of valuable goods. Fundamental to these relationships is that the perception of the value of the good determines the perception of what is valuable labor. Not many people skilled in the manufacture of birch-bark canoes find employment these days.

It was the view of the steel workers that the plant, products, and profits for the owners were the result of their labor, which established for them an ownership right in their jobs and the plant. In reality, the plant and the jobs of the steel workers who worked there only existed because the principals of Carnegie Steel perceived profit opportunities and successfully found markets for the products of the plant. It was Carnegie, Frick, and their partners whose entrepreneurial and managerial efforts had made the Homestead mill an economically viable manufacturing entity. Absent the success of those efforts, the plant and its physical contents would sit unused no matter what amount of labor was present.[19]

Economic analysis also supports Andrew Carnegie's view that the price of steel products and labor markets should determine steel workers' wages; it does not support the view of the Homestead steel workers that wages should determine prices.[20] Wages do not determine the prices of a profitable firm; rather, it is profitable firms that are able to offer employment and pay wages. The tragedy of Homestead is that a mob of ignorant and brutish men and women took destructive actions against an employer, its property, and guards hired by the firm, in the misguided belief that they were morally and factually in the right. This turned them into criminals and, for many of them, destroyed their lives and left them and their families destitute. Bad ideas can and do have serious material consequences.

Chapter Seven

Empire Builder

At the beginning of 1893, the partners of Carnegie Steel Company, Ltd., were in an enviable position. Their company was now the largest and most profitable steel maker in the world and holder of a majority interest in the largest coke producer in the United States, shipping more than half of all coke made in the United States (Warren, 1996, p. 167). Carnegie's plants produced rails for the railroad industry; structural shapes and steel beams for bridge building, elevated railways, and skyscraper construction; armor plate for the Department of the Navy; and many other less important, but still vital, iron and steel products. Even in the strife-torn year of 1892, the company made a profit of $4 million on its total capitalization of $25 million.

At fifty-seven years of age, Andrew Carnegie's majority share of the partnership would seemingly represent the pinnacle of success that any man could expect to reach in a lifetime. And yet the decade of the 1890s would bring an expansion of the company that raised profits to $21 million in 1899, $40 million in 1900, and an estimated $50 million for 1901—the year Carnegie would sell the firm to J. P. Morgan for almost half a billion dollars (Hendrick, 1932, vol. 2, p. 53). In the process, Carnegie Steel would engage in a program of massive vertical integration and worldwide sales expansion. Although the Panic of 1893 would severely affect the fortunes of other business organizations, the years 1893–1897 would be ones of expansion for Carnegie Steel. Indeed, gross tons of steel ingots produced in all Carnegie Steel plants rose from 863,027 in 1893 to 1,686,377 by 1897, and 2,663,412 in 1899 (Bridge, 1903, p. 297). This simply reflected the results of Carnegie's basic investment philosophy as he continued "improving his plants, scrapping obsolete equipment, installing the most modern machinery, acquiring ore fields on an enormous scale, building railroads, founding steamship lines, and developing an executive staff of the highest type" (Hendrick, 1932, vol. 2, p. 4).[1]

Three basic ingredients are needed for the steel-making process—iron ore, coke, and limestone. Carnegie Steel's majority ownership interests in the Frick Coke Company and the Pittsburg Limestone Company provided assured supplies of the latter two materials. Meaningful vertical integration would require the same assured supply of the iron ore that limestone, coke, and the furnaces turned into steel. Wall (1970, pp. 587–612) tells best how this was attained. The following is a brief summary of his detailed and exciting narrative.

Low-phosphorus ore suitable for the Bessemer process had been found in the Marquette Range in Michigan's Upper Peninsula in the 1840s, but ore deposits there were being rapidly depleted. What the industry required for continued growth was more sources of that ore, plus sources of lower-grade ore that could be used in open-hearth furnaces using the Thomas process. By the 1880s, the Menominee Range near Green Bay, Wisconsin; the Vermillion Range in Northern Minnesota near Lake Vermillion; and the Gogebic Range in Minnesota's Upper Peninsula and crossing the border into Michigan had been discovered and were being worked. The discovery of the ore in the Mesabi Range in the mid-1880s, located south of the Vermillion Range and west of the city of Duluth, was to eclipse them all in importance. The most important figures in developing the Mesabi were the four sons and three nephews of Lewis Merritt and, following them, Carnegie's boyhood friend Henry W. Oliver, and then John D. Rockefeller.

The Merritt family arrived in Duluth, Minnesota, in the 1850s. The brothers and cousins were originally interested in lumbering, but the patriarch of the family—Lewis Merritt—became convinced that the Mesabi hills concealed large amounts of iron ore. Led by Leonidas ("Lon") Merritt, Lewis Merritt's sons and nephews found large ore deposits close to the earth's surface in 1885 that could easily be mined using steam shovels. This would tremendously reduce the costs of extracting the ore as compared with deep-shaft mining. Tests showed that the ore was of a high grade with minimal phosphorus content; however, it existed in the form of a fine powder (hematite) that was viewed as difficult, if not impossible, to smelt given existing furnace technology. In addition, the ore deposits were in the deep woods at least fifty miles from any railroad line.

Nevertheless, the Merritts began accumulating leases on large tracts of land containing these ore deposits and searched for the capital funds needed to build a spur line from the planned mines to connect to the Duluth and Winnipeg Railroad. Doing so would provide transport for the ore to the city of Duluth on Lake Superior, where it could be shipped to steel manufacturers by way of the Great Lakes. Optimistically, Lon Merritt went to Pittsburgh in the spring of 1891 in an attempt to attract Henry Clay Frick's interest in the project, but he was unsuccessful. The Merritts then sought (and found) other ways of financing the construction of the spur, and shipments of ore from their Biwabik Mountain Iron Company to Duluth by rail were being made by 1892.

Despite their success in raising the funds necessary to mine the ore and build the rail spur, they were now deeply in debt and experiencing great financial difficulties. Fortunately for them, news of the furious prospecting activity in the Mesabi had spread and attracted the attention of Henry Oliver, who was in Minneapolis as a delegate to the 1892 Republican Convention. Oliver had his own furnaces to feed with ore in his Pittsburgh plow and shovel factory (Harvey, 1928, p. 188), and he quickly bought a partnership in the Merritts' mining operation. That done, Oliver went to Pittsburgh to talk with Frick.

Carnegie was initially opposed to any deal with Oliver and argued against the proposed investment. He considered his boyhood friend mercurial and reckless in his business judgment. Also, at this time Carnegie was exploring ore deposit possibilities in West Virginia. As it would later turn out, Carnegie was mistakenly judging the man instead of the likely success of the project itself. The West Virginia ore would also later prove to be noncompetitive with low-cost Mesabi deposits. Frick was only able to secure Carnegie's approval of a deal with Oliver and the Merritts by recasting its terms. Rather than directly investing in the Oliver/Merritt partnership, Frick was able to secure Carnegie's agreement for a $500,000 loan to it. This loan would be extended to the partnership in return for a 50 percent interest in the company for Carnegie Steel and a mortgage on their ore properties.[2]

Unfortunately, the Panic of 1893 struck when the credit-financed expansion of ore mining in the Mesabi was at its height. The Oliver/Merritt partnership not only owed Carnegie Steel but also had many other creditors, and it was in deep trouble as a result of the decline in ore demand caused by the recession. By this time, the Merritts were working six mines and had the additional financial burden of debts on their railroad and on loading docks that the firm had constructed in Duluth. The Merritts now set their sights on John D. Rockefeller as a possible investor. Rockefeller already owned some iron ore properties in the Gogebic range, in Cuba, and in Michigan and Minnesota. At first he rebuffed the Merritt overtures. Although he wasn't interested in their mines, he did buy first mortgage gold bonds of their railroad because it was being used to ship ore to Oliver and to Carnegie Steel.[3]

Finally, in late summer of 1893, Rockefeller entered into a contract that folded the six Merritt mines, the railroad, the ore docks, and Rockefeller's ore holdings into the Lake Superior Consolidated Iron Mines Company. The Merritts got company stock, while Rockefeller got first mortgage bonds. Oliver's and Carnegie Steel's mining companies were not part of the deal. By 1895, Rockefeller would gain majority control of Consolidated and continue to add greatly to its ore properties in the Mesabi.

The general public saw this activity as implying a pending and bitter rivalry between Rockefeller and Andrew Carnegie, although both men were actually on such friendly terms that they exchanged Christmas presents. Nevertheless, it was thought that Rockefeller's ore purchases were surely intended to provide an ore supply for a planned steel-making venture. Feeding the rumor mill were Rockefeller's actions in building his ore-carrying Bessemer Steamship Company so that he could transport the ore from his mines on the Great Lakes during the seven months of the year that they were ice free. However, the truth was that even though he now owned the richest iron ore deposits in the world, John D. Rockefeller had no interest in entering the steel manufacturing business in competition with Carnegie Steel and the other steel manufacturers. His goal was to control their ore supplies and the transportation network needed to get those supplies to them.

Regardless, Rockefeller's acquisitions unnerved Carnegie and Frick because of their potential to create a dominating position for Rockefeller in sources of ore and rail transport of ore to Duluth, and then by lake steamer to customers like Carnegie Steel (Nasaw, 2006, p. 515). Seeing an opportunity to broker a deal, Henry Oliver managed to mediate between Rockefeller and Carnegie. The result was a December 1896 agreement between the Rockefeller and Carnegie interests for a fifty-year lease on the Rockefeller ore-mining properties. Carnegie Steel would pay a royalty to Rockefeller on every ton of ore mined, as well as to ship it and the Oliver mine ore to a port near Cleveland using Rockefeller's railroads and his lake steamships. Rockefeller gained the royalties on ore taken from his mines and the shipping revenues for its transport by rail and boat. Carnegie gained an assured source of ore for his mills.[4] Cleverly, Carnegie withheld his consent until Oliver agreed to allow Carnegie Steel to increase its ownership of the Oliver Iron Mining Company to five-sixths, the increase to be paid out of profits.

Even with the ore from the Oliver and Rockefeller mines locked into his supply, Carnegie needed even more ore, and Oliver was soon securing other leases in the Vermillion and Gogebic ranges. Despite Carnegie's and Frick's misgivings, he convinced them to buy mines they could not lease. This was done by using the retained profits from the armor shop at Homestead for the purchases (Misa, 1995, p. 158). In arranging these leases and purchases, Oliver had the support of Charles Schwab, who had become Carnegie Steel president in 1897 (Misa, 1995, p. 163).[5] The result of all of these efforts, coupled with prosperous Carnegie Steel's ability to expand during recessions, was that, by September 1897, Carnegie Steel was self-sufficient in iron ore as well as in coke and limestone.[6]

There remained the problem of transporting the ore from the port on Lake Erie to Carnegie's plants south of Pittsburgh. Carnegie was fed up with the higher shipping rates that the PRR charged his company as compared to what his competitors paid. Their lower freight rates gave them a clear cost advantage for ore and coke transport (Wall, 1970, p. 613). The solution was for him to build a railroad from the Lake Erie port of Conneaut, Ohio, to the steel works. Fortunately, Frick had already had rail lines built to connect all the firm's plants in Pittsburgh and the Monongahela Valley. The resulting Union Railway was "a masterly conception; for it unified the scattered works and made them as easy to operate as if they had been contiguous, [giving them a] direct connection with every important railway system in Western Pennsylvania" (Bridge, 1903, p. 256).

To connect the lake port to his works, Carnegie bought the old and ramshackle Pittsburgh, Shenango & Lake Erie Company, a line that ran from Conneaut south to Butler, Pennsylvania. He had the line rebuilt and constructed an extension further south across the Allegheny River by means of a new bridge and so through Pittsburgh to connect with the Union Railway. This connection was made in the fall of 1897, and Carnegie Steel began running ore trains from Conneaut to the company's blast furnaces in Braddock, Duquesne, and Pittsburgh (Bridge, 1903, pp. 270–71). Renamed the Pittsburgh, Bessemer & Lake Erie Railroad, Carnegie successfully used its existence, the threat to build a further line to Connellsville, and his knowledge of his competitors' lower freight rates to compel a reduction in freight rates by the PRR (Wall, 1970, p. 618).

The penultimate step in completing the vertical integration of Carnegie Steel was the purchase and refitting of the docks at Conneaut. This Carnegie Steel did in 1898. The remaining problem was lake transport. Rockefeller's steamers could only transport half the tonnage of ore that Carnegie Steel now required. Once again, Henry Oliver stepped up to the plate. Acquiring six ore vessels from the Lake Superior Iron Company, Oliver Mining and Carnegie Steel organized the Pittsburgh Steamship Company (Wall, 1970, p. 623). Carnegie Steel then had major control of its products from mines to finished product and would continue to do so until its sale to J. P. Morgan in 1901. Misa (1995, p. 164) attributes this foundation for the merger of Carnegie Steel into U.S. Steel to "Oliver's strategic vision, realized through Schwab's support and Carnegie Steel's armor profits," although the merger itself was the realization of the strategic vision of Charles Schwab, as shall be shown.

Carnegie Steel's armor plate profits, used to buy iron ore mines in the Vermillion and Gogebic ranges, came from a series of contracts obtained by Carnegie to produce armor plate for the Department of the Navy. Rails produced in his Edgar Thomson mill in the early 1880s were cheaper than those produced by the Bethlehem Iron Company, forcing Bethlehem to diversify its production away from rails. When Joseph Wharton assumed control of Bethlehem in 1885, he erected an armor and heavy forging plant. In 1886 the U.S. Congress authorized the naval department to build an ordnance factory using purchased domestic steel. Subsequently, a $4 million contract was awarded to Bethlehem for armor plate for warships. When Bethlehem fell behind in delivering the order to the navy, then-secretary of the navy Benjamin Tracy turned to Carnegie (Misa, 1995, pp. 97–102).

At first Carnegie refused because of his pacifist views; however, by the late 1880s, he had overcome his objection to the extent that he sent Charles Schwab to Europe to look at plate mills and approved building such a mill at Homestead.[7] Now willing to manufacture armor for the purpose of defense, in 1890 Carnegie Steel bid for and was awarded a contract for six thousand tons of nickel-steel armor (Warren, 1996, pp. 143–44).[8] The armor plate contracts of the 1890s made up for the continued decline of demand for rail. Unfortunately for the two firms, competitive bidding decreased profits on armor contracts, so Carnegie and Bethlehem cut a pooling deal to bid $450 a ton and split contracts between the two firms.[9] Wall (1970, p. 649) estimates the actual cost of production as closer to $150 a ton than the $175 estimate that Charles Schwab made for the manufacture of one special order.[10]

Although profitable, armor plate production was not without its perils. In the late summer of 1893, a lawyer representing four Homestead armor workers approached Henry Frick and offered to sell evidence of fraud in the armor plate department. [11] Frick refused to pay, and the lawyer went to Secretary of the Navy Hilary A. Herbert with what would now be termed a "whistleblower" case. Herbert appointed a special board of investigation, which found Carnegie Steel guilty of fraud for specially treating the armor plates presented to naval inspectors for testing. The Bureau of Ordnance recommended a fine of 15 percent of the cost of armor purchased during the 1892–1893 period in question. Carnegie appealed to Secretary Herbert, and then to President Grover Cleveland, who reduced the fine to 10 percent, a matter of $140,489.44. In addition, Carnegie Steel had to pay 25 percent of the penalty to the four informers—another $35,121.23 (Wall, 1970, pp. 650–52; Nasaw, 2006, pp. 466–67).

Despite these conflicts with the Department of the Navy over costs and quality, they had no effect on the awarding of lucrative future armor plate contracts to Carnegie Steel. Also offsetting the decline in steel rail revenues were those from supplying beams and structural shapes for skyscraper construction in Chicago, for New York elevated railways, and for the Brooklyn Bridge. Additional revenue was obtained from the sale of steel parts to the Schoen Pressed Steel Car Company. In 1898–1899, Carnegie even tried to convince his partners to begin the manufacture of rail cars, but after long consideration the idea was dropped. The silver lining in Carnegie's cloud was that in early 1899, to keep Carnegie Steel from becoming a competitor, the Pressed Steel Car Company agreed to buy all its steel plates, angles, bar beams, channels, and axles from Carnegie Steel at a fixed price for a ten-year period. In addition, Schoen, who had once naively hoped that he would get a $400,000 loan from Carnegie, now had to pay him $1,000,000 in $100,000 yearly installments simply for Carnegie to not manufacture cars (Wall, 1970, p. 657).

For many industrial giants, the period of the 1890s was financially tumultuous. However, with the exception of the armor plate dispute with the Department of the Navy, this was not true at Carnegie Steel Company, Ltd. Profits rose steadily from 1893 until the sale of the firm in 1901. The main source of tumult in Carnegie Steel during that period of its vertical integration and output differentiation was within management—quarrels among partners and conflicts between Andrew Carnegie and Henry Clay Frick in particular. Despite the fact that "Carnegie always claimed that the most valuable asset his group of companies possessed was the quality of their men, especially of those at the top" (Warren, 1996, p. 207), and despite the high regard he had for the managerial talents of Frick, clashes between the two starting in the 1880s would reach a crescendo in the decade of the 1890s.

In 1886 and 1887, Carnegie had forced Frick to settle with striking coke workers so that steel production would not be interrupted. This action had angered Frick so much in 1887 that he resigned the presidency of his company, only to be wooed back by Carnegie six months later. The Homestead lockout and strike of 1892 had exacerbated the personal friction between the two men, mainly because of the self-promoting actions of Carnegie in his attempts to place the blame for the tragic events on Frick's decisions and actions and to dodge any responsibility for himself.

It could only have made matters worse when, in 1894–1895, Carnegie clandestinely, and unsuccessfully, attempted to arrange a merger of Frick's coke company with that of W. J. Rainey, Frick's largest competitor. Carnegie had even suggested that the combined companies be renamed the Frick-Rainey Company, an act that infuriated Frick (Wall, 1970, p. 734). Regarding Rainey, Frick said he was a "thief" and a "rascal," and he threatened to resign the chairmanship of both companies when he heard of the proposed deal, demanding that Carnegie buy out his interest in the steel company. The compromise reached on January 11, 1895, was that Frick remained chairman of both companies and John G. A. Leishman was appointed to the new post of president of Carnegie Steel. Five percent of Frick's 11 percent ownership share in the company was purchased and transferred to Leishman (Warren, 1996, pp. 215–19). This enabled Frick to pay off the notes he had given in purchasing his partnership interest and left his ownership share completely unencumbered (Harvey, 1928, p. 186).

For some years, Carnegie and his family had spent the period from May to October abroad. Most of their time was spent at rented castles in Scotland, where the Carnegies entertained guests and he hunted, fished, golfed, and generally played the part of a feudal lord or grandee. From May 1897 to October 1898, the Carnegies prolonged this stay, wintering on the Riviera. His wife, Louise, had given birth to their daughter, Margaret, in March and now wanted a permanent home in Scotland. Carnegie subsequently purchased the site of the ancient castle Skibo in far-northeast Scotland, with its thousands of acres of land, and began to build his own castle that summer (Wall, 1970, pp. 688–89; Nasaw, 2006, p. 564). During this period he also indicated in correspondence with his partners that he was open to retirement if they could either buy him out or sell to a third party. [12]

After Carnegie's return to the states that fall, two events occurred that together would bring Frick and Carnegie into serious conflict and produce the final break in their professional and personal relationships within little more than a year's time. The first was a meeting between the two in which Frick verbally agreed to a three-year contract price for coke sold to Carnegie Steel by the Frick Coke Company that was below current and expected future market prices. When Carnegie informed Henry Phipps of the deal, Phipps raised the question of what to do if coke prices fell. At this time Charles Schwab was president of Carnegie Steel, having succeeded John Leishman in April 1897 after Leishman fell out of favor with Carnegie and was forced out. Carnegie instructed Schwab to have Frick put a clause in the coke contract covering the contingency of a declining price. Frick's reaction to this suggestion was to tell Schwab that the verbal agreement was a mistake because neither he nor Carnegie possessed the authority to make such contracts. He said that it was up to Schwab and Thomas Lynch, the president of Frick Coke, to settle the question. Although Schwab subsequently reported Frick's response to Carnegie, nothing further was done about the matter at the time (Wall, 1970, pp. 734–35).

The second agreement between Carnegie and Frick that would contribute to a complete break between them took place at a meeting in December 1898. At that time, Carnegie told Frick that he was ready to retire and that Frick could explore the two options they had previously discussed in their correspondence. Frick and Phipps and the other junior partners vastly preferred the option of selling to an outside party. The discussion with Carnegie had led to an agreement of a sale price of $250 million for Carnegie Steel and $70 million for Frick Coke, for a total of $320 million if sold to an outside party. Finally, all those years of reduced dividends, enhanced capital investment, and undercapitalization would bring a rich reward to all partners, Carnegie included, if a sale at that price could be made.

Unfortunately, the only possible purchasers at such a price appeared to be the Federal Steel Company—newly formed by a J. P. Morgan syndicate—or John D. Rockefeller. Rockefeller proved to be uninterested, and Federal Steel was only interested if the purchase could be made with a stock issuance, a means that neither the Frick/Phipps faction nor Carnegie would accept (Warren, 1996, p. 230). The alternative, a reorganization of the two companies into one with a higher capitalization, was being explored separately by both the Frick/Phipps faction and Carnegie in early 1899 when Frick and Phipps found a new possibility for outside purchase at the $320 million price. Two notorious stock speculators, William H. Moore and his brother James Hobart Moore, backed by John W. ("Bet a Million") Gates,[13] were the potential purchasers. Knowing Carnegie's negative views of the trio, Frick and Phipps informed Carnegie that a syndicate that preferred anonymity at present was prepared to accept a ninety-day option for the purchase.

Carnegie's suspicious response was to request a $2 million cash deposit in trust, to be forfeit if the required capital was not raised by the ending day of the option. His ownership share of the companies would entitle him to $1,170,000 of the deposit if it was forfeit, with the rest going to the other partners according to their ownership shares in the two companies. To their dismay, Frick and Phipps were only able to obtain $1 million of the deposit from the syndicate and had to pledge the remaining $170,000 themselves, or Carnegie would not have agreed to the option. As Phipps and Frick had done, the junior partners all agreed to waive their own deposit share percentages of the $2 million in order for the deal to go through. What Frick and Phipps did not tell the other partners was that part of the deal would be a bonus for the two of them of $5 million for securing the option. After Carnegie sailed away to Europe on April 26, the option papers were signed by all parties involved, with Frick and Phipps using Carnegie's power of attorney on his behalf.[14] They then cabled Carnegie, not only informing him of the identities of the syndicate members but also including the details of the bonus arrangement.

Carnegie was outraged at both the deceptive actions and the self-dealing of Frick and Phipps, but he was unable to do anything about it at that point. Fortunately for him, as the summer wore on and the option expiration date of August 4 approached, it became apparent that the Moore syndicate would not be able to raise the capital to complete the purchase. A key speculator in the Moore syndicate and president of the largest Wall Street brokerage firm, former New York governor Roswell P. Flowers, had died on May 12. The effect of his death on financial markets was great enough that this event, and their notoriety as speculators, left the Moore brothers unable to raise the necessary funds (Hessen, 1975, p. 102; Nasaw, 2006, p. 562; Wall, 1970, p. 731; Warren, 1996, p. 235). Despite the pleas of Frick and Phipps for an extension, which they made in person to Carnegie at Skibo Castle, it was not granted. Carnegie kept the entire $1,170,000, although he had previously sent a note to the Carnegie Steel Board of Managers that said, "Of course any part paid by my partners I shall refund."[15]

As outraged as Carnegie had been on discovering that the Moore brothers were behind the syndicate and Frick and Phipps effectively part of it, both Frick and Phipps were equally outraged by Carnegie's apparent mendacity and his vengeful retention of their $170,000. Whether this episode would have been the turning point in Frick's future relations with Carnegie will never be known, because the coke price controversy, which had been smoldering in the background all year, burst into flames upon Carnegie's return to New York in October.

In the year since Carnegie and Frick had made their verbal agreement that coke would be sold to Carnegie Steel at $1.35 a ton, a price slightly below the then-market price, coke market prices had more than doubled. Lacking a final decision regarding the status of the agreement, Frick Coke began billing Carnegie Steel at higher and higher coke prices. Schwab's reaction was to pay the higher prices but mark the excess over the $1.35 as "payment on advance accounts only." On Carnegie's return home in October, he demanded that his and Frick's agreement be enforced and that the excess payments be refunded. The Frick Coke Board of Managers met on October 25 and passed a resolution denying the existence of any such agreement. [16]

Further inflaming the clash between Carnegie and Frick was Frick's purchase of a piece of land in the spring of 1899. [17] This was the 260-acre Wylie property on the bank of the Monongahela, six miles south of the Homestead plant, and for which Frick paid $635 an acre. In June 1899, when Carnegie Steel was considering locating a tube plant on that piece of property, Frick offered it to the company for $3,500 an acre (Warren, 1996, p. 247). At the Carnegie Steel Board of Managers meeting of November 6, it was decided that it was worth buying, either to prevent another steel company from using it or possibly for later Carnegie Steel expansion. [18]

While not quarreling openly with Frick at the meeting, Carnegie later remarked to junior partners that he was considering setting up a coking operation in competition with the Frick Company. He also criticized Frick for selling the Wylie property to his own partners in Carnegie Steel at a profit, implying that Frick had violated his fiduciary duty to the firm. To Frick, he reasserted the claim that their coke agreement stood. Frick's response to these comments was to appear at the November 20 Carnegie Steel Board of Managers meeting and read a blunt statement. In it he objected to Carnegie's attempt to dictate an unprofitable price of coke to the partners of the Frick Coke Company and to his threats to go into competition with them and ruin them financially if they didn't yield to his coke price demand. Frick also defended his purchase of the Wylie property as a decision made before it was apparent that it would be useful to Carnegie Steel.[19]

On December 4, Carnegie requested Frick's resignation as chairman of the Board of Managers of Carnegie Steel. Frick resigned the next day. The Carnegie Steel Company board then met on January 2, 1900, and voted to transfer enough Frick Coke Company shares held by Carnegie Steel to eight Carnegie partners so that they would be eligible to vote in Frick Coke's January 9 annual meeting. At that meeting, those present voted to increase the Frick board from five to seven members and then voted on the membership. Frick and President Lynch were reelected, but Carnegie's cousin Dod Lauder and four other Carnegie Steel board members were elected to form a majority. The Carnegie majority then voted to retain Lynch as president, to eliminate Frick's office of chairman of the board, and in favor of a formal contract to supply Carnegie Steel with coke at $1.35 a ton.

At a meeting between the two men in Frick's office the next morning, Carnegie threatened to use the Carnegie Steel partners' "Iron Clad" agreement to force Frick to sell out his 6 percent interest in the company at book value if Frick refused to accept the coke contract and took legal action. Frick's response was to call Carnegie "a god damned thief" and to drive the intimidated steel magnate out of the office.[20] The issues at this point were what legal action would be taken by Frick and what was the actual status of the so-called "Iron Clad" agreement of 1887, and its iterations from 1892 and 1897, on which Carnegie relied as a means of forcing Frick out.

The original "Iron Clad" agreement had been drawn up after Tom Carnegie's death and Andrew Carnegie's serious bout of typhoid fever in the fall of 1886. Fearing the financial consequences for both Carnegie, Phipps & Company and Carnegie Brothers if Carnegie had died and the firms had to settle with his estate, Henry Phipps and Carnegie had an agreement drawn up in January 1887. It provided for an extended buyout at book value of the partnership share of any partner leaving either firm. It also provided a means to force a partner out with a three-fourths majority interest vote. Because he held the majority interest in both firms, Carnegie was unaffected by the latter clause. All current partners were required to sign the agreement (Wall, 1970, pp. 490–92).

The reorganization that resulted in the Carnegie Steel Company in 1892 had also included an updated "Iron Clad" agreement. Over the years a number of partners had been bought out, either voluntarily or involuntarily, some receiving sums in addition to their book value. By 1897, it was apparent that even an extended buyout at book value of Carnegie, as well as other senior partners, would have had serious financial consequences because of the by-then greater capitalization of the firm. The agreement was modified a second time to allow for a longer period payout for buybacks. Phipps would not sign the new agreement. Because he had signed the original 1887 agreement, it was thought that his failure to sign the new one didn't matter. Phipps's view of the situation was that the purpose of the "Iron Clad" agreement was to keep the junior partners in line—the managers who had yet to pay off the debt for their shares. It did not apply to senior partners. Phipps, Carnegie, and Lauder had not signed the 1892 agreement for that reason. Under pressure from Phipps, Carnegie included an explicit statement of senior partner exclusion in the 1897 revision.[21] Nevertheless, Phipps found other parts of the agreement unjust and consequently would not sign it (Harvey, 1928, pp. 252–53).

Even before the tumultuous events of January 1900, Carnegie had decided to use the "Iron Clad" agreement against Frick. In order to be prepared for an anticipated fight the next day with Frick, Carnegie had called a meeting of the Carnegie Steel Board of Managers on January 8, 1900, to which Frick was not invited. At the meeting the board passed a resolution deeming the 1897 agreement a "supplemental agreement" and declaring that, in view of Phipps's failure to sign it, it was rescinded. The next day, the takeover of January 9 occurred at the annual meeting of the Frick Coke Company, and the day after that brought the clash in Frick's office when Carnegie threatened to invoke the "Iron Clad" agreement if Frick did not agree to the $1.35 a ton coke price. From that meeting, Carnegie hurried back to another Carnegie Steel emergency board meeting, where the members "passed a resolution invoking the Iron Clad and asking Henry Clay Frick 'to sell, assign and transfer to Carnegie Steel Company, Limited all of his interest in Carnegie Steel Company, Limited by 31 January 1900'" (Wall, 1970, pp. 753–54).

In a memorandum to Frick on January 17, 1900, Phipps claimed that "in each of the forms of that agreement—1887, 1892, and 1897—the provision for compelling partners to withdraw and to sell their interests to the company specifically excluded senior partners who fully owned the interests credited to them, that is, who were not in debt to the company for their share" (Warren, 1996, p. 262).[22] It was Phipps's view that Frick was thus protected despite the threat from Carnegie to force the sale of his partnership share.

Frick lost no time in reacting to Carnegie's threat. He and John Walker (a former Carnegie, Phipps executive and recently displaced Frick Coke board member), joined by Henry Phipps, decided to file two lawsuits. One would seek to enjoin Frick Coke from the sale of coke to Carnegie Steel at $1.35 a ton, while the other "would be to force a fair evaluation of Frick's interest in Carnegie Steel or to bring about a liquidation of the company's assets and a dissolution of the company" (Wall, 1970, p. 755). Hiring one of the most distinguished Philadelphia lawyers to represent them in these suits, Frick and his co-plaintiffs presented their equity suit brief to the Court of Common Pleas of Allegheny County.

Meanwhile, the Carnegie Steel board passed a resolution on January 24 accepting the coke contract of $1.35 a ton with Frick Coke for five years, retroactive to January 1, 1899, and requiring a refund from Frick Coke of $596,000 for previous overcharges. At this time the market price for coke was $3.50 a ton (Bridge, 1903, p. 329). On February 1, the board passed a resolution that transferred Frick's 6 percent interest to Carnegie Steel, to be held in trust.

In preparing to meet Frick's objections to the terms of the "Iron Clad" agreement, Carnegie's lawyers discovered two unwelcome facts: the 1892 agreement had never been signed by all the partners, and the 1887 agreement was among partners of the two companies that had been merged into Carnegie Steel in 1892 and no longer had any legal existence. Having voted to rescind the agreement of 1897, the board of Carnegie Steel had relied on the two earlier agreements to use against Frick, and they both were suddenly problematic. The whole arrangement now stood on extremely questionable legal grounds.

Frick's suit, which he filed in early February, together with Carnegie's response, filed in early March, revealed to the public for the first time the exorbitant profits of Carnegie Steel and its ridiculous undercapitalization. The 1899 profits of $21 million and expected profits for 1900 of $40 million on a capital value of $25 million suggested an extraordinary, even scandalous, return on capital for the firm.[23] There was a firestorm of public criticism, especially from the Democratic press, in a period when industrial trusts were already under attack. This line of criticism was compounded by the fact that those profits had been produced under the protection of tariffs passed by Republican-dominated Congresses. Currently in office and running for re-election was President William McKinley, a Republican and the namesake of the "McKinley Tariff." Carnegie and Frick began to receive tremendous private pressure from other industrialists, as well as prominent figures in the

Republican Party, to reach some compromise that would take the conflict out of the public arena.

Added to this pressure was the very real possibility that if Carnegie won the suit by getting the court to accept the book value of the firm, he would never be able to sell it anywhere near its expected value of $250–300 million. And if that happened, the value of Frick's partnership share would be nowhere near what he knew it to be. As Wall (1970, p. 762) points out, the situation would be even worse in the event of a Frick victory. Then the firm would be liquidated at whatever the physical assets would bring on the market, and the reward for Frick and Carnegie would be even less. The result was a meeting on March 22 in Atlantic City, where it was agreed that the Carnegie Steel Company, Ltd., and the Frick Coke Company would be merged into a new company of which they would be divisions. It would be named the Carnegie Company, capitalized at $320 million, with the partnership interests the same in the new company as they had been prior to the merger, though the value of those interests was now greatly enhanced. In return, both suits would be dropped and Frick's position relegated to that of shareholder. The "Iron Clad" agreement became history and the Board of Managers became the Board of Directors, with Charles Schwab as president of the newly formed company (Hendrick, 1932, vol. 2, p. 110).

Wall (1970, p. 764) characterizes Carnegie's actions in this affair as motivated by "principle," while those of Frick were motivated by "money." His reasons are that Carnegie was responding to the challenge to his authority posed by Frick, whereas Frick had used the "Iron Clad" agreement when it suited him and abandoned it when he was financially threatened by it. There is another interpretation, however, not so favorable to Carnegie.

Profits for Carnegie Steel had risen $1 million each year from 1893 until 1896. When John Leishman was forced out in early 1897, the 1896 profits of $6 million on a capitalization of Carnegie Steel of $25 million—a 24 percent return on capital—were high, but nothing like the $11.5 million of 1898, the $21 million of 1899, or the expected $40 million of 1900 that would raise so much public criticism. Leishman's 5 percent partnership would have brought him $1.25 million in 1897 according to the "Iron Clad" terms.

Even before Leishman's buyout, there were buyouts of other partners at above-par amounts, particularly William Abbott (Warren, 1996, p. 266).[24] Even earlier, in 1879, when William Shinn was forced out of the Edgar Thomson Steel Company, his threat of a lawsuit resulted in Carnegie paying him a premium of 100 percent for his shares (Wall, 1970, p. 358). Also, the last buyout of partner John Pontefract on January 3, 1899, had been done with Carnegie's insistence on an additional honorarium because "we might have other Estates to deal with, and a precedent might be troublesome" (Wall, 1970, p. 751). Presumably, what Carnegie meant was that Pontefract's buyout at par, with an artificially low capitalization of the firm, might raise issues of fairness and financial exploitation in view of the previous year's profit of $11.5 million, or 46 percent on invested capital. The situation would become potentially more troublesome over the next two years.

And yet Carnegie threatened to buy out Frick at par, knowing how grossly unfair his treatment would appear as compared to that of Pontefract, or even Abbott. Add to this Carnegie's historical emphasis on cost-cutting whenever possible, as well as the consequent forced contract on Frick Coke of $1.35 a ton at a time when market prices were above $3, and a motive in addition to a challenge to his authority suggests itself—money. Carnegie Steel stood to gain a great cost advantage over its competitors with such a low price for coke, and this at the expense of the junior partners of the Frick Coke Company. Carnegie Steel's majority partnership in Frick Coke would give it the same low returns as the other Frick partners on sales to Carnegie Steel, but the benefit to Carnegie Steel's own profits would more than cancel that out. As it is said, one hand washes the other. The partners in Frick Coke, other than Carnegie, were to be once more sacrificed to the needs—and profits—of the partners in Carnegie Steel. Also, with Frick bought out at par, Carnegie would have even more largess to dispense with a recapitalization and sale of the firm.

On Frick's side of this argument was certainly a desire for money. This was shown by Frick's and Phipps's deal with the Moore brothers' syndicate for a $5 million bonus for securing the option to buy Carnegie Steel and Frick Coke. It is also shown by Frick's purchase of the Wylie property for $635 an acre only to sell it to Carnegie Steel a few months later for $3,500 an acre. Yet Frick's actions must also have been motivated by anger at what Carnegie proposed to do to him, to John Walker, and to the junior partners of Frick Coke by forcing them to sell coke to Carnegie Steel for less than half the market price. Added to this would certainly be almost twenty years of business association, during which Frick built Carnegie's empire with energetic and successful hands-on management while Carnegie summered in Scotland, only to have Carnegie attempt to shove him out the door with less than a third of his share of the real value of the two firms.

Whatever the actual motivations on either side of their dispute, the two men never met again after Frick chased Carnegie out of his office on January 10, 1900. It is said that years later, when they were both living in mansions on the East Side in New York City, Carnegie sent Frick a note by messenger suggesting that they resume a social relationship. Frick's message back to Carnegie was "Tell Mr. Carnegie that I'll meet him in Hell" (Wall, 1970, p. 764).

It is notable that there is little mention of Henry Clay Frick in Carnegie's autobiography, despite their many years of close association and Frick's yeoman services in building Carnegie's empire of steel. Carnegie briefly praises him as "a man with a positive genius for [the Frick Coke Company] management" (1920, p. 108), as seen at the time that Carnegie purchased majority ownership in Frick's company. A mere sixteen pages later there is a mean-spirited reference to a conversation Carnegie says he had with one of his nonrioting roller employees in the fall of 1892 after Carnegie's return to Pittsburgh (Carnegie, 1920, p. 124). To Carnegie's statement that the company's offer should have been accepted, the roller replies, "Oh, Mr. Carnegie, it wasn't a question of dollars. The boys would have let you kick 'em, but they wouldn't let that other man stroke their hair." This episode supposedly illustrates Frick's "lack of due appreciation and of kind treatment of employees" (a behavior not characteristic of Carnegie himself, of course).

The two years prior to Frick's departure from management had seen a lot of mergers in the steel industry of firms that made finished products, such as tubes, hoops, wires and barbed wire, and structural beams. A syndicate headed by John W. Gates and William and James Moore had organized the American Steel and Wire Company, the American Tin Plate Company, the American Sheet Steel, and the American Steel Hoop Company (Wall, 1970, p. 767). Billets to produce these products were purchased from Carnegie Steel (the largest producer), J. P. Morgan's Federal Steel Company, and the Moore brothers' National Steel Company. From 1898 to 1900, these three producers had a price-fixing agreement to prevent competition; however, in the face of a declining demand for fabricated steel products in 1900, Federal and National began to cut prices and expand their own production of steel billets. Carnegie had no interest in seeing the market for his output reduced and decided to counter their moves by expanding into the production of finished products.

He knew that his steel production facilities were superior to Morgan's and those of the Moore brothers, and his dominance of the Carnegie Company meant he didn't have to pay dividends like they did to their public owners. His ability to plow the major part of his profits into capital investment made his competitors vulnerable to his expansion into their markets (Hendrick, 1932, vol. 2, p. 120). In 1898, Frick had appointed a committee to consider building a pipe and tube plant at Conneaut, Ohio (Bridge, 1903, p. 358). In the summer of 1900, Schwab was ordered to plan a line of fabricating plants. The first of these would be a steel tube plant at Conneaut Harbor, using a new method that would produce seamless tubes at $10 a ton less than was possible with the old method of bending sheet steel into a tube and welding the seam (Hessen, 1975, p. 112).

A press release to *World's Work* announced the Carnegie Company's plans for building a $12 million tube plant at Conneaut. Subsequently, Carnegie was quoted in the January 17, 1901, *Iron Trade Review* as saying that the new plant was necessary because J. P. Morgan's National Tube Company was now making its own billets instead of buying them from Carnegie. In addition, the doubling of his freight rates by the Pennsylvania Railroad made desirable a plant on Lake Erie, where finished product could be transported by water or competing rail (Bridge, 1903, p. 360). The higher rail rates were the work of Alexander J. Cassatt, the new head of the PRR, who ended the practice of secret rebates to Carnegie Steel that had kept Carnegie's transportation costs lower than they otherwise would have been, and at the expense of PRR stockholders.

Carnegie also responded to the higher rail transport rates by planning to expand his own rail network. If he could connect his Pittsburgh, Bessemer, and Lake Erie and his Union Railway lines to the Western Maryland Railroad Company, he could ship directly to Baltimore. In addition, the Western Maryland was part of the George Gould syndicate's plan to extend a rail network from Baltimore through Pittsburgh to St. Louis (Wall, 1970, pp. 774–80). A new tube plant at Conneaut on Lake Erie that would receive its iron ore by water and its coke and lime by Carnegie's rail network, added to rail connections that could take Carnegie products east to the port of Baltimore or west from Pittsburgh to St. Louis and then north, south, or west—this would be serious competition for other producers of finished steel products.

In the spring of 1899, Carnegie Steel had hosted a group of New York bankers in Pittsburgh to show them a new steel vault that had been built for Union Trust Company. They were also shown around the company's steel works (Bridge, 1903, p. 362). On December 12, 1900, J. Edward Simmons, president of the Fourth National Bank of New York, expressed his gratitude by hosting a dinner at the University Club in honor of the Carnegie Company's then president, Charles Schwab. There were eighty bankers and businessmen in attendance, including Carnegie and J. P. Morgan. Carnegie left early to speak at another meeting, and Schwab was asked to say a few words. Instead, he spoke for forty-five minutes, outlining his vision of a monopoly steel firm with specialized plants located all over the country. With no competition and plants located where their products were sold, costs and prices would be considerably lower than at present and profits higher. He argued that "if the steel industry were made as efficient as possible, if its plants were specialized, integrated, and centrally managed, and if its leaders were willing to cooperate for long-range mutual growth, then an ever-widening market for steel could be created," with increased uses for steel found and new technologies for its production developed (Hessen, 1975, p. 116).

J. P. Morgan was sufficiently impressed with Schwab's address to speak at length with him after the end of the dinner. A few weeks later brought an invitation to Schwab from Morgan for dinner in New York. The dinner with Morgan and two of his partners turned into a discussion at Morgan's home that lasted until 3 a.m. the next morning. Morgan's position was that he did not want to buy out Carnegie—just prevent his expansion into finished steel products—while Schwab argued that only a buyout followed by his retirement would stop Carnegie. The discussion then moved to the question of how Schwab's vision of an integrated steel industry could be turned into reality. At the end, Schwab was asked to put the details in a memorandum that included a list of the companies that would have to be bought to create such a megafirm (Hessen, 1975, p. 117).

This he did, and it was presented during another marathon meeting with Morgan and John Gates a few days later. Morgan must have been captivated by Schwab's vision because, at the end of the meeting, Morgan asked Schwab to speak to Carnegie about selling and get him to state an offer price. One can only wonder if the participants in those two meetings were able to keep straight faces as they discussed this scheme. It went far beyond the concept of pools or cartels to embrace the planning of a centrally managed monopoly steel producer, much like the dreams of state socialists, but privately owned rather than being a government operation.[25]

Schwab was either naïve or duplicitous in suggesting that the end result would be both lower prices to consumers and higher profits to producers. Governmentally owned firms are historically renowned for their constantly rising costs and prices, absent any competition from the private sector. There's no reason to think that a private monopoly would act any differently. In fact, publicly regulated but privately owned "public utilities" are notorious for constantly rising costs of operation used as arguments for increasing rates to obtain a "fair" return on capital invested. Absent public regulation or any significant competition, and protected by tariffs on imported steel products, the result could be profit-maximizing monopoly prices for such a firm.

The purpose of the pools and cartels in the American steel industry had been to eliminate price competition and portion out markets for steel and steel products to existing steel producers in order to maintain, or even increase, their profits. Those "gentlemen's agreements" had always broken down when declining demand or actual recession pressured the weaker members to break their agreement and cut their prices. Carnegie had prospered by breaking agreements when it suited him, as well as by taking advantage of his large retained earnings to expand his capital investment during recessions, incorporating the latest technology and reducing his costs of production. Now his firm—the largest steel producer in the country—was intended to be the cornerstone of the merger of the industry.[26]

In late January 1901, Schwab spoke with Carnegie after a golf game at the St. Andrews Golf Club in Westchester County. He related the events that had occurred after the dinner on December 12 and asked Carnegie whether he had a price at which he would sell. Carnegie replied that he would have to think it over and asked Schwab to call the next morning for a decision. Indeed, Carnegie had much to consider regarding any deal with J. P. Morgan, given what Morgan had done to him only sixteen years earlier.[27]

At that time, Carnegie was involved in a dispute with the Pennsylvania Railroad over an increase in its freight rates. He became aware that the PRR was also involved in a scheme to bring competition to the main line of the New York Central Railroad with the PRR's New York, Buffalo, and West Shore Railway line along the west bank of the Hudson River. William Vanderbilt of the New York Central was planning to retaliate by building a line that would compete with the PRR's main line in southwestern Pennsylvania. Carnegie, Henry Phipps, and several other Pittsburgh-area manufacturers invested $5 million in Vanderbilt's new South Pennsylvania Railroad. Construction began in the summer of 1884.

Unfortunately for the enterprise—and for Carnegie—J. P. Morgan was a member of the board of the New York Central. More important for his own interests, Morgan was a broker of bonds for both the New York Central and the PRR and an owner of New York Central stock, currently in decline as a result of the news of the coming West Shore competition. He desired no competition between the two railroads. Using his influence on the New York Central board, he arranged a meeting aboard his yacht in July 1885 between George Roberts, president of the PRR, and Chauncey Depew, president of the New York Central. The outcome was an agreement to transfer control of the West Shore line along the Hudson to the New York Central and ownership of the South Pennsylvania line to the PRR.[28] From Carnegie's point of view, Morgan and the New York Central had stabbed him in the back and delivered him up to the continued control of the PRR.

This may have made it difficult for him to consider Morgan's offer to purchase the Carnegie Company, but when Schwab called the next morning Carnegie named a price of $400 million for Carnegie Company and all its holdings.[29] Perhaps taking precautions against any possible Morgan duplicity, he also stipulated that his, Lucy Carnegie's, and Dod Lauder's share of the payment would have to be made in first mortgage, 5 percent gold bonds. When Schwab took this offer price to Morgan, it was immediately accepted. Although the purchase contract was initially only a verbal one, followed a few days later by a fifteen-minute meeting between Carnegie and Morgan at which they shook hands on the deal, the contract was approved on February 4 by the Carnegie Company board. A February 26 letter from Carnegie formalized the contract to sell Carnegie's interest in his company to the newly incorporated U.S. Steel.

Carnegie, Lucy Carnegie, and Dod Lauder received $304 million in first mortgage gold bonds, while the rest of the partners in the new steel company received a total of $1.1 billion in preferred and common stock in U.S. Steel in return for their ownership interests in the previously existing firms now merged into one.[30] Those firms included the Carnegie Company, the National Steel Company, the American Steel and Wire Company, and the American Tin Plate Company. The first billion-dollar corporation in the world was now a reality, with Carnegie's personal share of the buyout of his interest in the Carnegie Company standing at $225,639,000 in par-value gold bonds secured by a mortgage on U.S. Steel's property (Nasaw, 2006, p. 587; Wall, 1970, p. 792).

Andrew Carnegie was no longer in the steel business, but he now had an assured income of more than $11 million a year to devote to long-planned philanthropic activities, even if he never sold one bond. In fact, the money flowed in so fast that by the time of his death in 1919, he had given away in excess of $350 million and still had an estate of $30 million to bequeath (Wall, 1970, p. 1042).

Chapter Eight

Philanthropist

In his December 1868 St. Nicolas Hotel memorandum to himself, thirty-three-year-old Andrew Carnegie expressed his dismay at the idolatry of money and vowed to devote all of his future earnings above $50,000 per year to charitable purposes (Wall, 1970, pp. 224–25). From that time on, his was to be a life of literary studies and public policy advocacy. Of course, this was not the career path Carnegie subsequently followed; instead, he devoted himself to building his income and wealth during the rest of the century, this apparent "idolatry of money" only ending with his retirement from business in 1901. Nevertheless, his philanthropic activities began decades before then.

Carnegie's earliest philanthropic act also included an element of self-interest. In the early 1860s, as a partner with William Coleman in their Columbia Oil Company, he would have participated in the decision to compete for the best Titusville workers by paying above-market wages and employing the latest equipment. In addition, the partners in Columbia provided family housing and a company library for their employees. Besides the obvious gain to the workers and their families from these nonwage benefits, the reputation they gave the company no doubt increased employment applications and decreased labor turnover, as well as providing incentives to greater labor productivity (Wall, 1970, p. 178).

The last listed benefit—a workers' library—was one especially dear to young Carnegie and would later become a common nonwage benefit for Carnegie workers. Despite his own meager four years of formal education in Dunfermline, he was raised in a literate family, several of whom were leading participants in the economic and political debates of the day. His father,

Will, had been an avid reader and borrower of books from the local Trades-man's Subscription Library, as were other relatives and friends (Wall, 1970, p. 38; Carnegie, 1920, p. 48). Later, as a young telegraph operator in Alle-gheny City, young Andy had benefited from free access to Colonel James Anderson's personal library for "working boys." When Anderson trans-formed it into "The Mechanics' and Apprentices' Library," Carnegie suc-cessfully lobbied to retain his own free access to what had grown to become a subscription library (Carnegie, 1920, pp. 35–47; Wall, 1970, pp. 106–9).

Thirty years later, in 1881, at the suggestion of Captain Jones, Carnegie would fund a reading room at his Edgar Thomson works. This was the first of many such reading rooms and libraries at Carnegie plants, intended to pro-vide his employees with the same free access to self-education and self-improvement that he had enjoyed. Ironically, strong opposition to Carnegie's library building project came from organized labor and the political left. Their view was that Carnegie had accrued his fortune at the expense of his workers and was wasting it on something of little benefit to them (Bobinski, 1969, pp. 102–4). So much for Carnegie's actions to open a door to self-improvement, however he may have acquired the wealth to do so.

Also in 1881, Carnegie would fund a free public library for Dunfermline. His mother even laid the cornerstone during a triumphant visit by mother and son to their original Scottish home (Wall, 1970, pp. 406–9). In terms that would become standard for his later gifts of library buildings, the grant was contingent on the expenditures on books and operational expenses being paid by the municipality, thus partially socializing Carnegie's private gift in order to give the town taxpayers a stake in its success (Nasaw, 2006, p. 193). Of course, a tax-supported library was only "free" in a pay-per-use sense. Unlike subscription libraries, the cost of use was not confined to the users. The taxpayers of the town were assessed the operational expenses; it was not "free" to them.[1] As is the case with taxpayer-supported government schools, those who make no use of the provided service are coerced to financially subsidize those who do.[2]

Not surprisingly, in addition to the opposition of organized labor to his later library gifting project, Carnegie faced other sources of opposition as well as problems endemic to every publicly provided service. In some cities there was political opposition to spending money on such projects or placing the city in the position of being the recipient of charity. In others, there was opposition to the idea of taxing to pay the operational expenses. Some wrongly believed that Carnegie required that his name be on the building and viewed this as a vanity project on his part.[3] Even after accepting the funds for a building, many small towns failed to support the operational expense or used the building for other purposes. However, despite the opposition he faced in some communities, the failure of others to financially support the buildings he had given them, and the misuse and misappropriation that sometimes occurred, Carnegie never regretted this project (Bobinski, 1969, pp. 87–102, 105–10, 161–70).

The Dunfermline library was not Carnegie's first gift to the citizenry of his birthplace. His formal beginning in philanthropy actually had occurred in 1874, when he gave $25,000 to his birthplace to build a public recreation and health club, including a swimming pool and bath complex—the "Carnegie Baths" (Nasaw, 2006, p. 185). In the decades to come, there would be many such buildings and institutions named after him in an unprecedented total philanthropic program of some $350 million.

If young Carnegie had already decided by December 1868 to engage in philanthropy, he needed guiding principles to rule his future philanthropic actions. In the June and December 1889 issues of the *North American Review*, a two-part article on "Wealth" appeared under Carnegie's authorship. This later became known as his "Gospel of Wealth," and the articles were reprinted many times under that name.[4] Carnegie begins with the optimistic assertion that "the problem of our age is the proper administration of wealth, so that the ties of brotherhood may still bind together the rich and poor in harmonious relationship" (Wall, 1992, p. 130). Although manufacturing has made it possible for "the poor [to] enjoy what the rich could not before afford," there remains a great gap between the wealthy few (such as Carnegie himself) and the penurious laboring many. Individualism, private property, the "Law of Competition," and the "Law of Accumulation of Wealth" have created this inequality in rewards at the same time that they created modern civilization and its vast social wealth, he opined (Wall, 1992, p. 134).

Rather than accept the arguments of socialists or anarchists to abolish property rights, and thus civilization and its material fruits, Carnegie argues that the solution lies in the wise administration of existing wealth by its possessors. To stimulate them to do so, he recommends confiscatory estate taxes. Ideally, men of wealth should "set an example of modest, unostentatious living," while "provid[ing] moderately" for their dependents. Most important, the man of wealth should consider all surplus revenues that come to him simply as trust funds, which he is called on to administer in the manner that, in his judgment, is best calculated to produce the most beneficial results for the community—the man of wealth thus becoming the mere agent and trustee for his poorer brethren, bringing to their service his superior wisdom, experience, and ability to administer, doing for them better than they would or could do for themselves (Wall, 1992, p. 138).

The guiding philanthropic principle that Carnegie recommends is "to help those who will help themselves" by means of founding public institutions of various kinds. As candidates for such giving, he lists the founding and/or support of universities, free libraries, museums, medical treatment and research facilities, art museums, concert halls, and church buildings, as well as the providing of public parks and recreational facilities. Regarding those who die still in possession of their fortunes, he says, "The man who dies thus rich dies disgraced" (Wall, 1992, p. 140).

In assessing Carnegie's words, one must begin by recognizing that he meant them. Before these words were written he had already given a recreational facility and a library building to his birthplace and funded reading rooms for his employees. He ultimately gave away all but $30 million of his vast fortune before his death in 1919, and he did so with the knowledge and consent of his wife. Their prenuptial agreement of April 22, 1887, explicitly provided Louise Carnegie with an annual income in return for her voluntary surrender of her rights to his estate so that, with her full support, he might "devote the bulk of his estate to charitable and educational purposes" (Nasaw, 2006, pp. 297–98).

That said, it must be acknowledged that Andrew Carnegie accumulated the great fortune that he gave away using a combination of extortion and entrepreneurship. The tariffs on iron and steel products that kept their domestic prices above international ones were extortions from the customers and general population in the domestic market for the products of Carnegie's iron and steel empire. The insider deals that he made with officers of the Pennsylvania Railroad and other business firms advantaged him and his partners at the expense of the stockholders of the firms whose business he thus captured. The pooling agreements in which he participated (until it suited him to break them) kept his customers' prices above those that competition would have set. Carnegie was also an active force in pressuring, and even bribing, congressmen to maintain iron and steel product tariffs, to his and his industry's advantage. He became a government contractor for armor plate and, in a pooling agreement with Bethlehem Iron Company, charged his fellow taxpayers a price that was three times his cost of production. In his own firms, he used his majority ownership to divert profits from his various partners to use as capital investment and unhesitatingly forced out some of them while paying them only book value for their consequently greatly undercapitalized partnership shares.

One must also recognize that despite protective tariffs and unscrupulous dealings with customers, politicians, and his partners over the years, Carnegie's entrepreneurial talents in developing new markets and innovating new technology cannot be downplayed. He was a fierce competitor, dedicated to decreasing his costs so that, when he chose to do so, he could undercut current market prices for the products he manufactured and sold and grow his share of those markets. He prided himself in providing the highest-quality products technologically possible at the time. He took risks in adopting new technology that other firms were too conservative or too timid to adopt until he had opened the way. He developed new markets for products, such as that of steel bridges to replace wooden ones, and the beams and structural shapes for the Chicago School of architects to use to build skyscrapers in Chicago. Nevertheless, the hubris of the "Gospel of Wealth" is undeniable. *Gospel* seems an appropriate term for such an arrogant and presumptuous pronouncement of the necessity of the "superior wisdom, experience and ability" of men of wealth being enlisted to benefit their less intelligent and capable brethren. This arrogance is intensified by the suggestion that all other "men of wealth" be coerced into Carnegie's program through the threat of confiscatory estate taxes. Carnegie's advice for these men of wealth to "set an example of modest, unostentatious living" is also wryly amusing considering his own historic behavior.

He first employed a servant in his family's large house in 1858 after the move to Altoona, Pennsylvania, as Thomas Scott's assistant. Carnegie's staff of servants would only increase as he moved from houses to mansions to Scottish castles over the coming decades. Young Carnegie's December 1868 memorandum to himself on future study and philanthropic plans was written while he was a resident of the most luxurious hotel in New York, the St. Nicholas. A few years later he and his mother would move to an even more luxurious one, the Windsor. After his marriage to Louise in 1887, he bought the former Huntington mansion at 5 West 51st Street, although for the next ten years he and Louise would spend five or more months of the year in rented castles in Scotland.

Andrew and Louise Carnegie had begun their custom of spending the summer months in Scotland following their marriage on April 22, 1887.[5] Their honeymoon was spent on the Isle of Wight, after which they traveled to

Kilgraston House, a leased country home twenty-five miles north of Dun-fermline. Desirous of a larger residence in which to entertain their family, friends, and other guests, the Carnegies spent the next decade of summers (with the exception of the summer of 1892) in the leased Cluny Castle. After the birth of their daughter Margaret in the spring of 1897, the proud new parents' desire for a permanent home led to an offer to purchase the castle from its owner, Cluny Ewen Macpherson. His unwillingness to sell posed a problem for the Carnegies. If they truly desired a comparable Scottish prop-erty for their vacations, they had to find another castle for summers following that of 1897.

The solution was the purchase from the Duke of Sutherland of a twenty-two-thousand-acre estate and mansion on the Firth of Dornach in Sutherland in far northern Scotland. The mansion itself sat on the site of ancient Skibo Castle, originally built in the early thirteenth century by Gilbert de Moravia, the archdeacon of Moray. The estate's most recent owner, Ewen Charles Sutherland Walker, Laird of Skibo, had suffered severe financial reverses after building the mansion and was forced by court administration of his resultant bankruptcy to sell the estate to pay off his debts. Carnegie's subse-quent actions to convert the mansion into a new Skibo Castle would add another $1.2 million of expenditure to the original $425,000 purchase price.[6] This involved adding new wings on the north, south, and west of the central mansion hall, as well as a private lake, a golf course, and an enclosed and heated saltwater swimming pool. An additional eighteen thousand acres bor-dering the River Shin was purchased from the Duke of Sutherland so that Carnegie could have a waterfall and better salmon fishing (Hendrick, 1932, vol. 2, p. 156). The end result was a forty-thousand-acre estate with a two-hundred-room vacation home requiring a staff of eighty-five servants during the Carnegies' summer residence. Farm buildings, lodge houses, roads, a dam on the River Evelix, and opulent furnishings for the castle complete the picture of an extensive playground and entertainment complex at which the Carnegies and their many guests could vacation. "Modest, unostentatious living" indeed!

One could add to the list of Carnegie homes his yacht, *Seabreeze*, and his various other residences, including the mansion he built at 2 East 91st Street (now the Smithsonian's Cooper Hewitt Museum); his country home near Greenwich, Connecticut; his weekend cottage at the St. Andrews Golf Club; his sixty-room mansion—"Shadowbrook"—near Lennox, Massachusetts; his travels throughout Europe and around the world; and, of course, his purchase of the Pittencrieff estate of the Hunt family at Dunfermline, which gave Carnegie the title of "Laird of Pittencrieff" and made it possible for him to turn the estate into a park for the town's residents.

Truly, Carnegie's exhortation in favor of unostentatious living must be taken with a large grain of salt; however, there is no denying what he did with the greatest part of the fortune he built as his industrial empire grew until swallowed into U.S. Steel. As one proceeds down the list of public institutional giving he recommended in the "Gospel of Wealth" and compares it with what he was actually able to accomplish, one can only marvel at how far his reach exceeded his grasp. The interest payments on his U.S. Steel bonds flowed in at so great a rate that he was physically unable to give away his fortune strictly in accordance with his "Gospel of Wealth" guiding principle. In the end, he was forced to use major amounts of it to endow institutions with much more general missions than universities, libraries, museums, and so on.

In 1919, the Carnegie Endowment for International Peace (founded in 1910 with a grant of $10 million from Carnegie "to hasten the abolition of international war") published *A Manual of the Public Benefactions of Andrew Carnegie*.[7] A summary statement on page 311 at the end of the book shows a total of $20,363,010.11 given by Carnegie to universities and colleges; $60,363,808.75 in 2,811 grants to build free public libraries; and $26,719,380.67 in total to endow and fund the Carnegie Institute in Pittsburgh, which included at its completion a museum of natural history, a music hall, a library, a library school, a department of fine arts, and a technological institute.

Carnegie had actually begun the last-mentioned project in the 1880s before writing his "Gospel of Wealth" and persisted in his efforts to create the institute until its foundation in 1896 with an initial endowment fund of $1 million. Even earlier, in 1884, he gave $50,000 to Bellevue Hospital for medical student laboratories (Nasaw, 2006, p. 240). In 1887, he gave $5,000 to the Pittsburgh Exposition Society to help fund a music hall (Nasaw, 2006, p. 326). And, of course, there was the building in New York of what became "Carnegie Hall" in the early 1890s when his net worth was estimated to be approximately $15 million and rising (Nasaw, 2006, p. 359).

The orchestral hall in New York that became known as "Carnegie Hall" was actually built as an investment that Carnegie intended and expected to be profitable; however, grand benefit to the city though it remains, it was one of his few investment failures. Organized as the Music Hall Company in 1889, with Carnegie as its senior partner, he soon found himself forced to cover its continuing deficits. In true Carnegie fashion, he finally bought the stock of the other partners at a 75 percent discount, although, in all fairness, it must be said that his financial contribution to the hall's existence was far greater than theirs (Schickel, 1960, pp. 29–31). Nonetheless, some partners in Carnegie ventures must have been forced to see the truth in the old adage that "he who sups with the Devil had better bring a long spoon."

Carnegie's philanthropic side showed itself early in his career in the form of relatively small donations and continued throughout his life. As his income and wealth grew, so did his philanthropic ambition. Following his retirement in 1901, the giving only accelerated. In 1873, Carnegie donated a church organ to the small Swedenborgian church that he and his father had attended in the early 1850s. By 1919, the Carnegie Peace Endowment's *Manual* (p. 311) shows he had given a total of $6,248,309 for 7,689 organs. Before his retirement, he gave a private pension in 1891 to T. T. Woodruff, the then-bankrupt and penurious founder of the Woodruff Sleeping Car Company. This was the company in which young Carnegie's early partnership interest had proved so lucrative, though not (eventually) for Woodruff himself (Wall, 1970, p. 211).

Soon after his retirement in 1901, Carnegie turned over more than $5 million of his bonds to Carnegie Company managers. Of that total, $1 million was earmarked to maintain the employees' libraries at Braddock, Homestead, and Duquesne, while $4 million was to be used to provide pensions for longtime employees and payments to those injured or the dependents of those killed (Wall, 1970, p. 826). By the end of his life, there were hundreds of people receiving private pensions from Carnegie, including Rudyard Kipling and Booker T. Washington (Wall, 1970, p. 823).[8] He even offered a pension to former president Grover Cleveland at a time when former presidents were expected to provide for themselves. Cleveland turned him down; however, Carnegie's will provided pensions for Cleveland's and Theodore Roosevelt's widows, and one for former president William Taft (Nasaw, 2006, p. 634; Wall, 1970, p. 1043).

In the mid-1870s, Carnegie gave $6,000 in five installments to Western University of Pennsylvania (now the University of Pittsburgh) (Wall, 1970, p. 815). As previously mentioned, by the time of his death he had given more than $20 million to colleges and universities, most of which were small institutions such as Tuskegee, Hampton Institute, and Berea College (Wall, 1970, p. 865).[9] In addition, Carnegie gave $10 million in bonds in 1901 to establish the Carnegie Trust for the Universities of Scotland. One half of the income from the bonds was to be used for the instructional fees for "students of Scottish birth or extraction" enrolled in St. Andrews, Aberdeen, Edinburgh, or Glasgow universities, while the other half was to be dedicated to the improvement of science and technological education at those universities. Considering that the combined total endowment of the four institutions at the time of his gift was a mere $360,000, this was an immense boon to them. The annual income alone from the bonds would be almost 50 percent greater than their whole combined endowments (Wall, 1970, p. 837).

One other great education-related gift by Carnegie was the founding in 1905 of the Carnegie Foundation for the Advancement of Teaching.[10] He did so because of his belief that "of all the professions, that of teaching is probably the most unfairly, yes, most meanly paid, though it should rank with the highest" (Carnegie, 1920, p. 268). Carnegie initially endowed the foundation with $10 million to be used to provide free retirement pensions for college professors at private, nonsectarian colleges and universities in the United States and Canada. In order to decide which private, nonsectarian institutions to include in the pension plan, the foundation trustees set a minimum endowment criterion and then evaluated the standards for admissions and graduation of the applicants. The result was that only one-fourth of the initial applicants were accepted. This was a shock to the whole higher education system in the country. Institutions included in the Carnegie pension fund were now more attractive to prospective faculty, students, and donors than those not included.

The most beneficial unintended consequence of this situation was that faculty at excluded institutions pressured their boards and administrations to break sectarian ties and raise both admissions and graduation standards in order to be included in the pension fund. As Wall (1970, p. 877) observes, "By 1909, it was quite apparent to anyone interested in higher education that the Carnegie Foundation had become the national unofficial accrediting agency for colleges and universities." The foundation added to this institutional pressure with further investigations, published critiques, and suggestions for standards. By 1919, financial demands on it required the Carnegie Foundation to be reorganized into the Teachers Insurance and Annuities Association, a defined contribution, retirement insurance nonprofit, rather than a free pension foundation. Andrew Carnegie and the Carnegie Corporation of New York had given it a total of $29,250,000 (*Manual*, 1919, p. 311).

The first few years of Carnegie's retirement were notable for several great philanthropic initiatives on his part. In addition to those already mentioned, he endowed the Carnegie Institution of Washington (1901), the Carnegie Dunfermline Trust (1903), the Palace of Peace at The Hague (1903), the Carnegie Hero Fund Commission (1904), the Central American Court of Justice and Pan American Union buildings (1908), and the Church Peace Union (1914). Most important was the endowment of the Carnegie Corporation in 1911 as a foundation intended by him to continue philanthropic activity following the guiding principle of his "Gospel of Wealth."

The mission of the Carnegie Institution of Washington, to which Carnegie gave more than $22 million, was an extension of Carnegie's interest in supporting the contributions to society made by universities and colleges. The institute was founded to promote basic research in science and publish the results (*Manual*, 1919, pp. 81–82, 98). Besides the various research departments and grants to outside scholars, it contributed funds to build the Mt. Wilson Observatory and also funded astronomical projects there, and it built and sailed a special nonmagnetic sailing ship, the *Carnegie*, with the mission of improving nautical charts of the world's oceans.

The Dunfermline Trust was an extension of earlier gifts given by Carnegie to the people of his birthplace. In addition to the library, baths, and other recreational facilities he had previously given the town, he now bought the nearby estate of Colonel Thomas Hunt, Laird of Pittencrief, and presented it to the town as a park. He only retained the part of the estate that contained Malcolm's Tower and the ruined palace of the Stuarts, thus obtaining for himself the title of "Laird." The trust was established to create and manage the sixty-acre park, recreational facilities, and other activities provided to the townspeople. In addition, it funded medical and dental care for the children of the town, a college of hygiene and physical education, a school of music, a craft school, and a women's institute. A total of $3.75 million was eventually given to the trust by Carnegie (Nasaw, 2006, p. 642; Wall, 1970, pp. 847–54; *Manual*, 1919, p. 311).

The Carnegie Hero Fund Commission was created in 1904 to benefit those who "are injured or lose their lives in attempting to preserve or rescue their fellows." The total endowment was $10.5 million by 1919. Not only individuals who survived but also communities suffering disasters and the dependents of "heroes" were beneficiaries of this favorite fund of Carnegie's (*Manual*, 1919, pp. 109–11, 311). He said that the founding of the fund was a "delightful" task, one "in which my whole heart was concerned," and "I cherish a fatherly regard for it since no one suggested it to me . . . it is my own bairn" (Carnegie, 1920, p. 253). In his eyes, it was to be chiefly a pension fund for living heroes or, if dead, their surviving families. Later, he endowed similar funds in most Western European nations, and his autobiography includes excerpts from letters to him from the American ambassador to Germany as well as from King Edward VII in praise of those funds. By 2004, the American fund had provided $27 million in awards in North America alone, and funds in many countries continue to operate today (Nasaw, 2006, p. 667).

In addition to his more narrowly focused philanthropic activities, Carnegie was a tireless opponent of war and promoter of international peace. Despite his history as a munitions manufacturer, he actively promoted international peace efforts and supported peacekeeping bodies even to the founding in 1910 of the Carnegie Endowment for International Peace.[11] Endowing it with an initial $10 million, Carnegie gave as its purpose "to hasten the abolition of international war, the foulest blot upon our civilization" (*Manual*, 1919, p. 165). Earlier, in 1903, he had provided $1.5 million for the construction of the Palace of Peace at The Hague, Netherlands. This was to house the Permanent Arbitration Court created by The Hague Peace Conference of 1899 for the settling of disputes, as well as a resource library of international law. Carnegie referred to the building as "the most holy building in the world because it has the holiest end in view" (1920, p. 285).

A building to house the Central American Court of Justice in Cartago, Costa Rica, and a Pan American Union Building to house that organization in Washington, D.C., were additional Carnegie gifts intended to promote the peaceful settlement of international disputes.[12] He also provided more than $2 million to advance the work of the Church Peace Union, which he established on February 14, 1914. It was intended to bring together representatives of churches in the United States, Europe, and Asia "to discuss how the churches of the world might work together for promoting international good will and establishing peaceful and judicial machinery to take the place of wars in the settlement of international disputes" (*Manual*, 1919, p. 264).

To this list must be added Carnegie's quixotic attempt to prevent the Philippine Islands from becoming a possession of the United States as one of the spoils of its victory in the 1898 Spanish-American War. He argued publicly that such an annexation would be costly and might lead to a Philippine war of independence against America. He then offered to pay the federal government the $20 million for the islands that the treaty required that Spain be paid in order that he could grant the inhabitants their freedom. That offer was not accepted, and his predicted consequences soon followed (Wall, 1970, pp. 694–95; Nasaw, 2006, pp. 544–45). What a grand philanthropic gesture that would have been—to buy and gift to it the political freedom of an entire population!

By 1911, Carnegie had given away $180 million and realized that, at the rate his remaining bonds were earning interest income, he would never be able to give them all away on the relatively small scale on which he had been operating. His friend, former secretary of state Elihu Root, suggested that he put the remainder in a trust, select a board of trustees, and give them the responsibility of continuing his philanthropy (Nasaw, 2006, pp. 766–67; Wall, 1970, pp. 882–83). The result was the founding of the Carnegie Corporation of New York, chartered in June and endowed in November 1911. After all the transfers were complete, Carnegie had endowed the trust with $125 million. At his death, $10,336,867 was added to that amount (Lagemann, 1989, p. 3).

According to the charter, the Carnegie Corporation of New York existed "for the purpose of receiving and maintaining a fund or funds and applying the income thereof to promote the advancement and diffusion of knowledge and understanding among the people of the United States, by aiding technical schools, institutions of higher learning, libraries, scientific research, hero funds, useful publications, and by such other agencies and means as shall from time to time be found appropriate therefore" (*Manual*, 1919, p. 201). An amendment dated April 23, 1917, extended the corporation's reach to Canada and the British colonies. Carnegie had already established the Carnegie United Kingdom Trust in 1913 with an endowment of $10 million to continue his program of library building, church organ gifts, and other charitable purposes there.

From its founding in 1911 until his death in 1919, the Corporation continued "to increase opportunities for the release and development of individual talent," as Carnegie had done with his previous individual giving and intended would continue to be done by his trustees (Lagemann, 1989, p. 6). After all, the key principle stated in his "Gospel of Wealth" is "to help those who will help themselves." Once he was safely dead, however, trustees Elihu Root (then president of the Carnegie Endowment for International Peace) and Henry Smith Pritchett (former president of the Massachusetts Institute of Technology and now president of the Carnegie Foundation for the Advancement of Teaching) successfully transformed the corporation into a policy-influencing institution for general social reform. As a result, "large institution building grants, intended to establish centers of public policy experts, became the order of the day" (Lagemann, 1989, p. 7).

This situation lasted until 1923, when trustee Frederick Paul Keppel became the dominating force on the board; he worked to change the corporation into an institution that "disseminate[d] traditionally elite culture to a larger number of people" (Lagemann, 1989, p. 7). The new focus continued until 1942, after which there was a return to the attempt to use the Corporation's resources to influence social policy. Lagemann argues (1989, p. 9) that the overall theme since Carnegie's death has been to use the corporation to support progress for humanity and to support government policies that are believed to be progressive. Looking back to the original charter, it would appear that the last phrase in the corporation's purpose statement opened the door to practically any mission that trustees might decide would "promote the advancement and diffusion of knowledge and understanding."

There is much irony in this situation: Carnegie had amassed a fortune from the general population through a combination of entrepreneurial alertness, innovation, and any means at hand—honest or otherwise—and then proceeded to dispense it according to his personal idiosyncrasies. His personally chosen trustees subsequently used the remains of that fortune in the same way—that is, as they saw fit. Carnegie's desire to help those who would help themselves was turned into a mandate for general social engineering.

At their last meeting, Henry Clay Frick had called Carnegie "a god damned thief." One can only wonder whether this inversion of Carnegie's intended use for a large part of the proceeds of that "thievery" would have amused Frick, who unfortunately passed away only four months after Andrew Carnegie died in his sleep on the morning of August 11, 1919.

Chapter Nine

A Summing Up

Andrew Carnegie built his industrial empire in an economic context shaped by the powerful influences of war, government-subsidized and -driven railroad building, prohibitive tariffs on iron and steel products, the revolution in building construction, and the late nineteenth-century military preparation for possible future wars. All of these influences were the result of the actions of other human beings, most of them beyond his personal control. They provided a stimulus to his entrepreneurship and innovation as he sought to produce the output of his various industries to satisfy the demand thus provided.

He also did what was possible to influence those who acted to provide that demand. He contributed to the lobbying and bribery that provided those protective tariffs, knowing full well that this enabled greater growth and higher prices for his companies. He formed agreements with his competitors to fix prices above where actual competition would have set them. He used his insider knowledge and contacts with those managing the Pennsylvania Railroad to channel the railroad's growth into the growth of his industrial ventures and personal fortune. Despite his expressed pacifist views, he became a military contractor and supplied armor for naval ships.

Nevertheless, within the economic context of his time he acted as a dynamic and effective entrepreneur. His alertness to profitmaking opportunities and early adoption of innovations put him in the forefront of his fellow industrialists within a relatively short period of time. He provided improved bridges and rails for the expansion of the railroad system and improved structural forms and beams for bridges and Chicago skyscrapers, and he introduced constant improvements in production organization and technique. Carnegie was an early adopter of the latest technology for the production of steel products and continued to increase his capital investments and innovations up to the time he retired from active business. His emphasis on metallurgical chemistry, together with capital investment in advanced production methods, transformed the methods of making iron and steel and improved the quality of products made of both metals.

In all this, Carnegie was a force for better coordination in the markets in which he competed. Increased output, produced at ever-decreasing costs and higher quality, provided to those who demanded it, and better adapted to the uses to which it would be put—these were all fruits of his labors and those with whom he chose to work. His very success in generating ever-increasing profits for Carnegie Steel, as compared to other steel makers, was a sign of the degree to which his efforts improved the market process for the industries in which he operated. This is not to slight the efforts of his key employees, such as Captain Jones, nor his key partners, such as Henry Phipps Jr. and Henry Clay Frick. But they were men he chose to work with because of his perception of their worth.

Every leading industrialist of that age—or ours, for that matter—was a mixture of virtue and vice, and Andrew Carnegie was no exception, as has been shown. He could be deceptive, mendacious, vindictive, or dishonest when it suited his purposes. The stockholders of the Pennsylvania Railroad, the people to whom he marketed bonds that he knew were subject to depreciation or default, and even his own partners became grist for his mill when he thought it was to his own advantage. When there was a conflict between the interests of the various companies in which he was the majority owner, he resolved it so that it gave him the greatest benefit. Most tellingly, his conduct after the Homestead Strike and during the final conflict with Henry Frick was reprehensible.

Yet, after he amassed his great wealth through fair means and foul, he gave almost all of it away. This was no grand gesture; it was done with serious intent and according to a principle and philanthropic guidelines expressed in his "Gospel of Wealth." Only the physical impossibility of doing so prevented him from personally supervising the complete distribution of that fortune according to his desire "to help those who will help themselves," as he had done. Exactly why he did this will never be known, but more can be said about the results of those actions.

The prohibitive tariffs of the nineteenth century on iron and steel products that enabled higher prices and profits for Andrew Carnegie and other U.S. steel makers diverted domestic resources, including labor, into the manufacture of iron and steel. Those resources were no longer available for other uses, whatever they might have been, either at that time or in the future. Protectionist legislation always channels resources away from their most productive uses either in the present or in the future, and it decreases the overall rates of economic growth and the rise in the overall standard of living of the affected population. Also, the higher prices charged by steel manufacturers because of the tariffs increased the costs of users of iron and steel, and so on to the final consumer. Protectionist legislation transfers wealth from consumers and all users of protected commodities to the protected industries and those who work in them.

The boom in the iron and steel industries, made possible by prohibitive tariffs, was strongly driven by the expansion of the country's railroad system. That expansion was heavily subsidized by government at all levels, and the rail companies were internally rife with corrupt financial practices. Many rail networks, including the main transcontinental lines, went bankrupt because of their expansion beyond the demand for their services, as well as internal corruption. That vast system in great part also represented a massive misallocation of resources from more productive uses. Those resources, including labor and iron and steel products, were poured into the less productive use of building an underutilized transportation system, as shown by the inability of many of the lines to be profitable. One can only speculate as to how and at what rate the U.S. economy otherwise would have developed absent a destructive war and the premature expansion of the railroad network, as well as the iron and steel industries. This is not to argue that the railroad and steel industries would not have eventually grown to be major assets of the burgeoning U.S. economy, but rather that they likely would not have grown as rapidly as they historically did under government stimulus and protective tariffs, and Andrew Carnegie would likely have had a smaller place in that history.

Andrew Carnegie amassed a great personal fortune as one consequence of the vast malinvestment in the nineteenth-century U.S. iron, steel, and railroad industries. He successfully took advantage of the context within which his entrepreneurship could produce that fortune. As mentioned above, within the context of his age he brought greater coordination to the markets from which he drew his resources and those for the products he manufactured and sold.

And yet there is a sense that the actions that produced the wealth that enabled his later philanthropy represented a diversion of resources from resource owners, taxpayers, bond investors, and customers prematurely into expanding railroad and steel production as well as into his own idiosyncratic philanthropic projects.

Notes

1. ENTREPRENEURIAL, ENTREPRENEURSHIP, AND ENTREPRENEURS

1. An extension of the Knightian theory into one of entrepreneurship as "judgment" can be found in Foss and Klein (2012).

2. A detailed and critical comparison of the respective theories of Kirzner and Schumpeter on entrepreneurship can be found in Bostaph (2013).

2. EARLY LIFE IN SCOTLAND

1. As a child, he was known as "Andra"; later in America it became "Andy." His family name was pronounced with the accent on the second syllable, which sounded like "neigh" (as in *neighbor*).

2. As an adult, Andrew Carnegie owned stock in several companies, but it was the dividends from their profits in which he was interested. In his autobiography, he views stock speculation as gambling and says, "Speculation is a parasite feeding upon values, creating none" (Carnegie, 1920, p. 154).

3. YOUTH IN WESTERN PENNSYLVANIA

1. Converting distant past dollar amounts to present equivalents is notoriously difficult and fundamentally misrepresentative. This is especially true since the Federal Reserve Act of 1913 ushered in the Age of Inflation—an era of the deliberate inflation of the money supply by the U.S. central bank from that time to the present day. This has created great difficulties in adjusting for price-level changes over great spans of time in order to compare past prices and

incomes with present ones. Also complicating such comparisons is the fact that the mix of commodities available changes constantly, as do their quality and their relative importance in daily living. There are even very strong arguments that the very concept of "the price level" is ambiguous. At any rate, in order to make sense of the price, income, and wealth numbers given in the present text, it may be helpful for the reader to know that computations of price-level change for the entire nineteenth century show that, despite fluctuation in times of boom, recession, or war, there was a decline in the calculated price level of about 2 percent over the entire century. In addition, although it also fluctuated, during that same span of time the average wage for adult male unskilled labor was approximately $1 a day. Perhaps this information may serve as a benchmark for a rough comparison of the increasing incomes and the rise to fortune of Andrew Carnegie from his initial $1.20 a week until his retirement in 1901 with a fortune of half a billion dollars or so.

2. David Nasaw notes (2006, p. 35) that O'Rielly had deliberately changed his family name from the usual spelling of O'Reilly, although Reid uses the conventional spelling in his history of the early years of the telegraph industry.

3. The first president of the Harrisburg, Portsmouth, Mt. Joy, and Lancaster Railroad was James Buchanan, later to become president of the United States. Also on the board of that railroad was Simon Cameron, Lincoln's first secretary of war (Burgess and Kennedy, 1949, p. 22).

4. It must be noted that White also described Scott as a man "not so much tainted by corruption as impregnated with it" (White, 2011, p. 4). The justification for this characterization will be presented later on.

5. The PRR retired its last wood-burning freight engine in 1862 (Stover, 1997, p. 148).

4. ON THE ROAD TO WEALTH

1. In his book *Railroaded* (2011), Richard White details the corrupt practices of financiers, men such as Leland Stanford and Collis P. Huntington, who built the transcontinental railroads. One of the ways they funneled money from the railroad companies to enrich themselves was by setting up insider companies to do the actual construction and overpaying for it. The Credit Mobilier of America scandal was one example of this practice and its results.

2. Morris (2005, pp. 95–96) points out that these investment and enterprise activities were "remnants from the pioneering company-building days of the 1840s and 1850s," when railroads "encouraged their executives to share investment risk in new technologies." Later, "risk sharing" morphed into "profit skimming." He also references Naomi Lamoreaux's work on information scarcity in the nineteenth century, when insider dealing provided signals to market participants in the absence of data.

3. The PRR was in the forefront of railroads in innovation. It imported the first steel rail from England in 1863; it was the first to adopt the Eli H. Janney automatic coupler; it early adopted the Westinghouse air brake; by 1870, it was experimenting with track tanks so a moving train could scoop up water; and it began lighting passenger cars with electricity in 1882 (Stover, 1997, pp. 145–54).

4. Flynn (1932, p. 129) remarks that the Pennsylvania Legislature "was called Tom Scott's legislature."

5. This is not to say that his judgment as an employer was affected by blood or friendship. As Casson remarks (1907, p. 125) of the many partners in the Carnegie companies in later

years, "Never before, in so prosperous a business, were there so few stupid relatives and favorites in places of authority."

6. The iron manufacturer may have been the Sun City Forge Company, in which Carnegie and Tom Miller were partners in 1861, according to Carnegie's autobiography. Miller and Carnegie also partnered in the Freedom Iron Company in early 1861. The Freedom Iron Company was reorganized in 1866 as the Freedom Iron and Steel Company (Wall, 1970, p. 259).

7. Carnegie's brother, Tom, and his frequent business partner, Tom Miller, would each later marry one of Coleman's daughters. Coleman was "one of the richest and ablest of Pittsburgh's iron masters" (Casson, 1907, p. 80).

8. Andrew and Anthony Kloman were German immigrants who first started business with a small forge at Ginty's Run in Millvale, a borough of Duquesne, where they forged axles for rail cars out of scrap iron (Bridge, 1903, pp. 1–3).

9. Henry Phipps Jr. was the younger son of Henry Phipps, the shoemaker for whom Margaret Carnegie had worked when Andy was a young teen in Allegheny City. His older brother, John, had been one of Andy Carnegie's boyhood friends but died accidentally at the age of eighteen. Henry Jr. became one of Tom Carnegie's friends and a key partner in Carnegie's industrial ventures.

10. It was Piper and Shiffler that built the Steubenville Bridge over the Ohio River, with its 320-foot-long main channel making it the first long-span railroad bridge in the United States (Jackson, 2001, p. 33).

11. Carnegie says 1863 in his autobiography (1920, p. 116). Hendrick (1932, vol. 1, p. 129) dates the reorganization as April 1865. Hendrick is probably correct for two reasons. One is given by Bridge's (1903, p. vi) characterization of Carnegie's narration of events in his autobiography as "the least trustworthy" of any. The other is the fact that in July and September 1865 both Thomson and Scott wrote letters of recommendation for the bridge company, which it then widely published to advertise its competence (Bridge, 1903, p. 50).

12. Pig iron was iron ore melted and with the oxygen driven out, to be replaced by carbon. It could be melted and cast into shapes in molds. Wrought iron was made by heating pig iron and removing the carbon by beating or rolling the iron (Temin, 1964, p. 16). Cast iron is stronger in compression, while wrought iron is strained because of its flexibility (Temin, 1964, p. 45). Cast iron is granulated inside, while wrought iron is fibrous (Bridge, 1903, p. 143).

13. Assuming an interest rate of 6 percent, which was not unusual for the time, this represented an income on an investment capital of almost $800,000. Carnegie was close to becoming a millionaire before the age of thirty.

14. Iron rails were made of wrought iron because of its resistance to strain and its flexibility in comparison to cast iron, which was better for structural shapes. Steel was made by heating wrought iron and adding carbon back into it (Temin, 1964, p. 19). The difference in durability between iron rails and those of steel was extreme. A steel rail "laid in the Camden goods station of the London and Northwestern line [in 1862] showed practically no wear [four years later] whereas iron rails laid alongside and subjected to precisely the same traffic had been broken up and replaced seventeen times" (Hendrick, 1932, vol. 1, p. 185).

15. As a result, the PRR could connect with the Atlantic and Pacific Railroad in St. Louis, another railroad that included Tom Scott and J. Edgar Thomson on its board of directors, "thus advancing Thomson and Scott's plans for a transcontinental railroad empire" (Jackson, 2001, p. 27).

16. Some idea of the extent to which Carnegie's business ethics may have been influenced by those of Tom Scott and J. Edgar Thomson may be gleaned from a memorandum he prepared for Scott and Thomson concerning a proposed Keystone contract for the St. Louis Bridge

superstructure. Keystone officers were willing to accept 10 percent above cost. Carnegie proposed that he, Scott, and Thomson contract with the Illinois and St. Louis Bridge Company to build the superstructure of the bridge for 20 percent above cost, and then subcontract with Keystone for 10 percent above cost. They would profit as agents for Keystone as well as from their ownership shares in that company. Carnegie and Thomson would also profit from the subcontract Keystone would have with the Union Iron Mills for bridge iron since Carnegie was the majority owner and Thomson held shares in it. How many more ways could there be for insiders to milk revenues out of a chain of subcontractors in which they held ownership shares? Well, here's another: Carnegie estimated that he and his associates, as shareholders, would garner $400,000 from the Keystone contract, so he also proposed that at least a part of their payment for the superstructure should be $1 million in bridge company stock. Because the bridge company was requiring its stock subscribers to pony up 40 percent of the stock's face value in cash, Carnegie and his two associates would be getting $1 million in bridge company stock for themselves while Keystone would be paying for it (Jackson, 2001, pp. 69–70).

17. The St. Louis and Illinois Bridge Company was first incorporated in 1855 by a group of Pacific Railroad of Missouri railroad men and southern Illinois businessmen ambitious for the commercial preeminence of St. Louis in the Mississippi River Valley. They were concerned about the possible loss of freight traffic to the bridge being constructed between Rock Island, Illinois, and Davenport, Iowa, by the Chicago and Rock Island Railroad. There were rival groups in Illinois that also sought the right to build a bridge at St. Louis from the Illinois side of the river. Nevertheless, after much political maneuvering in Missouri, Illinois, and the U.S. Congress, a reorganized St. Louis and Illinois Bridge Company eventually prevailed as the "Illinois and St. Louis Bridge Company" through a July 20, 1868, act of Congress. Actual construction of the St. Louis "Eads" Bridge began in the summer of 1867 (Jackson, 2001, pp. 3 and 55).

18. Carnegie's skepticism concerning Eads's competence as a bridge designer and constructor led him to sell his stock in the Illinois and St. Louis Bridge Company in late 1871. This was well before the bridge's completion and the subsequent bankruptcy of its parent company from lack of sufficient traffic to generate the revenue to pay its debts and operating costs (Nasaw, 2006, p. 135).

5. A MAN OF STEEL

1. According to Casson (1907, p. 36), "The first colonial iron works of any importance was established at Lynn, Massachusetts, in 1642."

2. See also Wall (1970, pp. 451–52) for Carnegie's argument for free trade in food on moral grounds but protection for industry on infant industry grounds. Carnegie's relative ignorance of economic principles, particularly international trade theory, is further illustrated by a statement in his 1898 article on "Imperialism" in the *North American Review*. In urging the United States to not put itself in the unfavorable position of other colonial powers by becoming one, he said, "If our country were blockaded by the united powers of the world for years, she would emerge from the embargo richer and stronger, and with her own resources more completely developed" (Wall, 1992, p. 303). There is no evidence in this statement of any awareness of the economic law of association, also known as the law of comparative advantage, which says that each person, state, or nation should specialize in producing those goods in which his or its relative productivity is greatest so that overall value productivity is the highest

attainable. Two or more persons, using a division of labor and specializing according to their respective comparative advantages, can produce more total economic value than both of them in isolation can accomplish. Autarchic production defeats the worldwide benefits of specializing according to comparative advantage by limiting the productivity of non-trading states or nations.

3. The "infant industry" argument fails for a number of reasons. One is that protection removes the incentive for the protected industry to emphasize cost reduction and innovation. Doing so successfully would remove the rationale for protection and reduce industry profits. With a tariff in place, industry prices can remain at or below the import prices produced by the tariff, regardless of the domestic cost of production. Taussig (1931, p. 56) remarks that production improvements in the iron industry were so slow to develop that railroad rails still had to be imported in the 1830s and 1840s. Another reason the "infant industry" argument fails is that the industry only exists and is able to obtain resources because of its protection against lower-cost foreign competitors and their lower prices. The resources it obtains are bid away from other domestic industries that are not in need of protection because they are competitive with foreign producers. By moving resources from more competitive to less competitive industries, the overall productive efficiency of the economy is reduced. The same argument applies to the protectionist plea to "protect American labor." Labor is the most versatile productive resource, and overall labor productivity is reduced by moving labor resources from higher-productivity to lower-productivity industries. The general point is that protectionism impedes the development of an economy's specialization according to its various comparative advantages in the production of commodities; it thereby misallocates resources and slows economic growth. It also penalizes all industries that use the protected industry's products by raising their costs, and, naturally, consumers of the higher-cost final products are hit in the pocketbook.

4. Of course, people do make mistakes in their trading activity as a result of ignorance, miscalculation, deliberate deception on the part of others, and so on. These errors cannot be representative of the outcomes of an exchange economy; if they were, chaos (rather than increased coordination of trading activities) would result. Increased coordination of the actions of profit-seeking individuals provided by the pricing system of an exchange economy is a key element in Friedrich Hayek's explanation of the market process. See O'Driscoll (1977) for an extended presentation of Hayek's paradigm.

5. Carnegie refers to himself as a "moderate" protectionist, being opposed to both high tariffs and free trade. Not having been instrumental in establishing tariffs on iron and steel imports, he claims to have always favored their gradual reduction and eventual elimination (Carnegie, 1920, pp. 142–48). Nevertheless, his firms contributed money to the American Iron and Steel Institute to pay for lobbying to keep tariffs high, and Carnegie himself made recommendations to members of both houses of Congress for tariffs on specific items (Wall, 1970, pp. 449–50). This included then-congressman William McKinley, who headed the congressional tariff committee in 1890. It probably helped Carnegie's case that he had given McKinley $5,000 in 1889 as a token of admiration (Nasaw, 2006, p. 376). Although tariffs on iron and steel were slowly reduced throughout the late nineteenth and early twentieth centuries, they were always high enough to be prohibitive in all but the most economically expansionist years.

6. Temin estimates (1964, p. 4) that more than one-third of "rolled iron and steel products made in America [for the twenty-five-year period 1860–1885] were rails." Carnegie did even better. According to Wall (1970, p. 348), "Over 90 per cent of [Carnegie's E.T. works] steel output in the period from 1875 to 1885 went into rails."

7. According to White (2011, p. 22), Thomas Clark Durant (Union Pacific) and Collis P. Huntington (Central Pacific) used $250,000 in Union Pacific bonds to bribe members of Congress to pass the Act of 1864. The icing on the cake was that most of the land given to the

railroads as subsidies was in Indian Territory. Thus, Native Americans were forced to subsidize the railroads that constructed the rails that would later be used to bring in the military troops to exterminate them.

8. The Bessemer process consists of blowing air through molten iron to remove the impurities, particularly carbon. Unfortunately, it did not remove phosphorus, and so required low-phosphorus ore. Abram S. Hewitt, later a congressman and then mayor of New York, "was the first American ironmaster to experiment with a Bessemer converter and to operate an open hearth furnace" (Krause, 1992, p. 62). Neither were commercial successes. The first commercial Bessemer steel made in America was produced by Edgar B. Ward in Detroit in 1864, and he rolled the first American-made steel rails at his rolling mill in Chicago in 1865 (Casson, 1907, pp. 16–17).

9. Wall (1970, p. 362 n.3) disputes Carnegie's contention (1920, p. 339) that he first became acquainted with Spencer's *Social Statics*, *First Principles*, *Data of Ethics*, and *The Descent of Man* as a youth in his Pittsburgh debating circle. Wall points out that Spencer's work was not widely known in the United States until the post–Civil War period, and it doesn't receive any mention in Carnegie's correspondence until after 1867. Given Carnegie's penchant for exaggerating his personal accomplishments in his autobiography, this was very likely the case.

10. Spencer's early work, especially *Social Statics*, implies a necessity—a teleology—in this process of development, although he does describe much of government activity as retarding social progress. Also, in the last part of the book, he says that the condition toward which mankind is progressing "is a condition toward which the whole creation tends" ([1851] 1995, p. 391). Later in the century, Spencer would disavow any implied determinism and allow for social retrogression under certain circumstances. See, in particular, *The Man versus the State* ([1884] 1969, esp. pp. 108–9).

11. These rights are to apply to all members of society on an equal basis, including women and children (Spencer, [1851] 1995, pp. 138–71). One can only imagine the reactions of male readers to this argument of Spencer in the male-dominated English world of 1851.

12. See also *The Man versus the State* ([1884] 1969, pp. 107, 113).

13. Carnegie's support for protective tariffs did wane over time as they became less and less necessary for his own firms. In a fall 1908 article in *Century Magazine*, he expressed his belief that they were no longer necessary for most imported goods. Restating the infant industry argument, he claimed that it had been successfully applied through policy, but tariffs now could be repealed. Democratic politicians were elated and Republicans outraged. The *New York World* ran a cartoon of Carnegie being chased by Republican Speaker of the House Joe Cannon and others bearing lynch ropes (Wall, 1970, pp. 960–64).

14. Hendrick (1932, vol. 1, p. 179) claims that Carnegie placed a total of $30 million in American bonds in Great Britain during the years 1867–1873. With his commission on the sales varying between 1.25 and 2.5 percent, this may have brought him between $375,000 and $750,000 in earnings in addition to those from his various investments and enterprises during this period (Wall, 1970, p. 285).

15. The name is due to the fact that it was there that British general Edward Braddock (1695–1755) was defeated in 1755 during the French and Indian War.

16. The rural location also made the land cheap and the taxes low compared to land closer to the city, while the river was a convenient source of water (Krause, 1992, p. 147).

17. As they had in past partnerships with Carnegie, Scott and Thomson remained silent partners, presumably because of the conflict of interests in their investment (Nasaw, 2006, p. 145). Both Wall (1970, p. 309) and Nasaw (2006, p. 143) reference the Articles of Co-Partnership, November 5, 1872, vol. 4, of the Andrew Carnegie Papers, Library of Congress, for the

list of partners; however, Wall—perhaps relying on Bridge (1903, p. 76)—lists Shinn as an original partner, while Nasaw does not. Nasaw also attributes ten shares, for an investment of $100,000, to McCandless, while Wall attributes only five shares and $50,000 investment to him. Shinn definitely was a partner by 1879, as shown by the fact that Carnegie had to buy him out at twice his investment to quash a lawsuit that Shinn had filed (Wall, 1970, p. 358; Nasaw, 2006, p. 208).

18. Of Andrew Carnegie's success in getting orders for the fledgling firm, Bridge (1903, p. 112) says, "Endowed with a ready wit, an excellent memory for stories, and a natural gift for reciting them, he became a social favorite in New York and Washington, and never missed a chance to make a useful acquaintance."

19. Before 1870, the steel rail duty had been 45 percent of declared value, which, at the current British price of $50 per ton, meant a duty of $22.50. Steel rail prices rose during the early 1870s, making the $28-per-ton duty a decreasing percentage; however, after 1873 prices began to fall until, by 1877, they were less than $28 per ton, making the duty more than 100 percent. By the 1880s, British prices were in the lower $30s per ton, while the U.S. price averaged in the lower $60s—quite a boon for Carnegie and other domestic producers of steel rails (Taussig, 1931, pp. 221–23).

20. By 1880, Holley "had designed six of the eleven Bessemer plants in operation in the United States . . . was the consulting engineer for three other plants, and his designs directly inspired the remaining two" (Krause, 1992, p. 70).

21. At this time the Siemens open-hearth furnaces were used in Germany, but not in England or America because of their high cost of operation in comparison to the Bessemer converter, although they produced a higher-quality steel. It was not until the late 1880s that open-hearth furnaces—which by then could use low-grade iron ore with high phosphorus content—became a viable rival to the Bessemer process. This was because it was discovered that the latter could be modified to use high-phosphorus iron ore with the Gilchrist-Thomas method, thus extending its usefulness (Wall, 1970, pp. 320–21).

22. The "Lucy" (named after Tom Carnegie's wife) was seventy-five feet high and twenty feet in diameter at its widest point (the "bosh"). In 1872, it was able to produce five hundred tons of iron a week; this had increased to one thousand tons by 1880 (Bridge, 1903, pp. 56–58).

23. Bridge (1903, p. 34) credits the E.T.'s cost manager, Henry Phipps, with being one of the first to use a chemist to test structural material so he could decrease the cost of production.

24. Casson (1907, p. 26) gives profits of $41,970.06 for the three months of 1875, $181,007.18 for 1876, $190,379.33 for 1877, $250,000 for 1878, $401,800 for 1879, and $1,625,000 for 1880. Given the recapitalization of E.T. Steel at $1 million after Coleman's departure and $1.25 million after the death of McCandless, this roughly agrees with Temin's (1964, p. 172) estimate of profit rates on capital invested in the E.T. works as 25 percent in the first full year of operation, 20 percent in 1877, and 30 percent in 1878. Return on capital invested would have been 130 percent in 1880. As Carnegie exclaimed in a letter to Shinn in August 1876, "Where is there such a business!"* (Wall, 1970, p. 320).

25. An industrial pool is a type of cartel, like the late twentieth-century Organization of Petroleum Exporting Countries (OPEC). Its members attempt to estimate the entire demand for their product, calculate the profit-maximizing price and total production quantity, and then assign a quota of output to each member—all of whom agree to sell at the same high price. Today, cartels are illegal in the United States, unless they are sanctioned by the federal government; in Carnegie's day, like insider trading, they were just another way of doing business. Cartels are inherently unstable unless their agreements are enforced, and prospective new entrants prevented, using political coercion. If the cartel is successful in maximizing industry profits by eliminating competition among the participating firms, this provides an incentive for

the creation of new firms and substitutes for the product. When possible, government coercion can be used to prevent the entry of new firms, but not much can be done to prevent the innovation of substitute products. There is also an incentive for members of a cartel to cheat on one another through clandestine price cuts and production in excess of the assigned quotas. After all, as the aphorism has it, "there is no honor among thieves."

26. Carnegie was intent on learning his competitors' costs by any means necessary, resorting to bribery if he could get them no other way (Wall, 1970, p. 520).

27. In his autobiography, Carnegie (1920, p. 135) says, "One of the chief sources of success in manufacturing is the introduction and strict maintenance of a perfect system of accounting so that responsibility for money or materials can be brought home to every man." Carnegie kept an eagle eye on all aspects of plant operation: "Supplied with daily reports of the product of every department of each of the [E.T.] works, he had leisure to make comparisons, and to prod with a sarcastic note any partner or superintendent whose work did not rank with the best" (Bridge, 1903, p. 113).

28. Carnegie seldom paid out more than 25 percent of profits as dividends, although he did pay out 35.7 percent in 1897 (Hessen, 1975, p. 71).

29. A rodman carried the leveling rod used by surveyors to lay out construction plans. Six months after he was hired at the age of seventeen by Captain Jones for this job in the plant's engineering corps, Schwab's ambition and intelligence earned him a promotion to chief engineer (Hessen, 1975, p. 16).

30. Even while on vacation, Carnegie's eyes were always open to learn new techniques and processes, such as the Dodd process for fusing steel facing to iron rails, or the most efficient shape of bells for blast furnaces, or the Thomas process for removing phosphorus from iron ore (Wall, 1970, pp. 233, 353, 405).

31. Of this, Bridge (1903, p. 113) says, "He had a mind free to range over the industrial field, picking up scraps of information concerning the requirements of railroads, and bringing news of many a large contract."

32. In 1874, the Pennsylvania legislature authorized the formation of limited liability companies, perhaps as one result of the Panic of 1873 (Bridge, 1903, p. 77).

33. Imports of steel rails fell precipitously from 1873 to 1875, were zero from 1876 to 1878, rose temporarily during the railroad boom of 1880–1882, and (except for 1887) were zero or negligible for the rest of the century (Temin, 1964, table C.14, p. 282).

34. According to Bridge (1903, p. 103), "Jones . . . never hesitated to throw away a tool that had cost half a million if a better one became available."

35. Jones's attitude toward his workforce may best be summarized in a quote from a February, 25, 1875, letter to E. V. McCandless: "The men should be made to feel that the company is interested in their welfare. Make the works a pleasant place for them" (Bridge, 1903, p. 82).

36. Note that the spelling of *Pittsburg* omits the *h*. Use of the *h* in the name was not standardized until late in the nineteenth century.

37. Formed in 1876, the Amalgamated Association of Iron and Steel Workers was a combination of the Sons of Vulcan—the puddlers' union—and the other skilled metalworkers' unions to make for a stronger bargaining unit in conflicts with management over wages (Nasaw, 2006, pp. 162–63). Bridge (1903, p. 153) attributes part of the labor problem at Pittsburg Bessemer to the fact that the converting works was controlled by Irishmen, while the rail mill was controlled by Welshmen, and general manager William Clark was a bitter antiunion foe.

38. According to Misa (1995, p. 65), two-thirds of the Chicago School of architects, including Louis Sullivan, had worked in Jenney's design office in the 1870s and 1880s.

39. The consultation relationship between Carnegie's bridge engineers and Chicago architects continued fruitfully through the 1890s. For example, it was a suggestion from a Keystone

Bridge engineer that was developed by Jenney and his associates in the mid-1890s into "a new structural design for bracing tall buildings against wind pressures" (Misa, 1995, p. 66).

40. Bridge claims (1903, pp. 172–73) that Frick's company went from one thousand ovens and three thousand acres of coal land in 1882 to ten thousand ovens, thirty-five thousand acres, and eleven thousand employees by 1889.

41. This also illustrates Israel Kirzner's point that capital equipment is only capital equipment so long as it is viewed as such. When other techniques are more cost effective, what was once productive equipment may become scrap. Obviously, Carnegie and Captain Jones understood that.

42. As previously mentioned, Schwab originally had been hired as unskilled labor by Captain Jones. Schwab had diplomas for surveying and engineering courses he had taken at St. Francis College in Loretto, Pennsylvania, when he was working as a clerk in a dry goods store located near the entrance of the Braddock plant. It was while working in that store that he met Jones. He quickly put that knowledge to use, as well as began an intensive study of steel making—even to the point of setting up a chemical lab in his house. By 1886, Schwab had been appointed general superintendent of the Homestead plant at the age of twenty-four. When Captain Jones was killed in 1889, Schwab became general superintendent at Braddock (Hessen, 1975, pp. 13, 15, 20, 27–29).

43. The Henry C. Frick Coke Company remained a separate corporation, and conflicts between it and Carnegie Steel would later prove an additional irritant for the Carnegie and Frick business relationship.

6. LABOR RELATIONS

1. Krause (1992, p. 112) points out that it was the lockout of 1874–1875 that stimulated the entry into Pittsburgh of the Knights of Labor as an organization intended to be a union of unions, thus making lockouts of particular unions more difficult. Another consequence of this labor dispute was the formation of the Amalgamated Association of Iron and Steel Workers in 1876 to unite the Sons of Vulcan, the Roll Hands, and the Associated Brotherhood of Iron and Steel Heaters, Rollers, and Roughers.

2. There was another brief lockout at Carnegie's Union Mills in 1879, which was quickly settled (Nasaw, 2006, p. 248). In contrast to expectations, given the conflicts of the period, from an examination of Carnegie's correspondence between his residence in New York and businesses in Pittsburgh during this period, Nasaw (2006, p. 177) concludes, "Carnegie paid little attention to his workers, their attempts at unionization, or their pay scales through most of the 1870s."

3. By 1891, Carnegie was arguing that the way to get a shift length change from twelve to eight hours in all of industry was for government to mandate such a change because "organized capital can beat organized labor." After all, he said, legislation already beneficially limited child and female labor (Wall, 1970, p. 392). A cynic might suspect that Carnegie's embrace of government fiat in this instance was a bit more self-serving than beneficent. From his experience during the decade of the eight-hour shift at the E.T. plant, he knew that competition between firms could financially penalize any single firm using eight-hour rather than twelve-hour shifts. His own firm finally was forced to go back to twelve-hour shifts in 1888 by such competition.

4. Bridge (1903, p. 192) notes that Carnegie was also concerned with the increased costs to his firms that would result from banking his blast furnaces. The longer a furnace was banked, the greater the danger that it would have to be relined—a costly process. Settling the strike kept revenue coming in and prevented costs from rising.

5. Frick also proposed selling out his ownership share in his company to Carnegie and his associates; however, Carnegie was too shrewd a judge of Frick's potential to accept the offer (Harvey, 1928, pp. 87–88).

6. In fact, Carnegie was not the first to introduce the sliding scale. Grand Master Miles Humphries of the Sons of Vulcan first negotiated the introduction of the sliding scale with Pittsburgh ironmaster B. F. Jones in 1865 (Krause, 1992, p. 94).

7. Note the difference in contract expiration dates for E.T. and Homestead. This favored the Homestead workforce because it meant that contract disputes would occur at a time of more favorable weather and likely busier plant production, imposing lesser costs of any work stoppage on the workers and more on Carnegie, Phipps.

8. Krause's sympathy with the strikers is illustrated throughout his 1992 chronicle of the various Homestead strikes in his continual use of terms like *black sheep* and *scabs* to describe men hired to replace striking workers. In his narrative, the Pinkertons and the men they escorted are "the enemy"; their attempt to enter the town is an "assault," while the steel workers are engaged in the "defense" of Homestead and their "republican values."

9. Bridge (1903, pp. 201–2) points out that the terms of settlement of the strike created two important sources of contention for future labor-management relations. The first was the question of how often the sliding scale of wages would be adjusted to output price changes, while the second was the newly empowered Amalgamated Association itself. Every department and sub-department now had a workers' committee whose officers attempted to control hiring, regulated all aspects of working conditions, and funneled even minor complaints up to management on a daily basis.

10. Despite the lockout, strike, violent struggle, and the hiring and training of replacement workers at Homestead from July through November of that year, corporate profits would only decline from the previous year's $4.3 to $4 million in 1892 (Morris, 2005, p. 358).

11. Frick made these two points in an article in the July 8, 1892, *Pittsburgh Commercial Gazette*, an excerpt of which is found in Demarest (1992, p. 27).

12. It is also apparent that Carnegie was expecting no agreement with the union on the new contracts because he contacted his cousin, George "Dod" Lauder Jr., in June, requesting that he begin recruiting English and Scottish machinists as possible replacement workers (Nasaw, 2006, p. 413). He also wrote Frick twice in June in support of Frick's hard negotiation stance (Wall, 1970, pp. 552–53).

13. The following outline of the actions of all parties involved in the "Homestead Strike" draws from the narratives of Burgoyne (1893, pp. 34–87), Bridge (1903, pp. 209–22), Hendrick (1932, vol. 1, pp. 389–96), and Krause (1992, pp. 3–6, 15–40, 311–14, 322). Differences in the accounts will be noted where appropriate.

14. Different sources give numbers ranging from thirty-three to fifty for the membership of the advisory committee. Krause (1992, p. 395) lists thirty-four members of that committee by name, including O'Donnell.

15. Bridge (1903, p. 213) and Krause (1992, p. 16) say that the first shots were fired at the approaching tug and barges and came from both the picket boats on the river and the crowd on the shore. Burgoyne (1893, p. 56) says that it is not known whether those shots were aimed at the barges or were just signals. There is no dispute that the first shots came from persons on the steel workers' side of the coming confrontation.

16. Krause (1992, p. 19) says that Heinde initiated the violence by slashing with a billy club at a worker named William Foy, who was blocking the gangplank and holding a cocked pistol. Then Heinde was clubbed by another worker, and both Foy and Heinde were shot. Whether a Pinkerton shot Foy before someone on shore shot Heinde is a matter of dispute. What is not disputed is that Heinde and his agents were prevented from landing on Carnegie Steel property by an occupying mob and that an exchange of gunfire followed the initial shootings.

17. In addition to these casualties, the Allegheny County coroner's records show three Pinkerton agents and seven steel workers dead from the fighting.

18. At this point in time the Pennsylvania National Guard was a trained and disciplined military organization. This was a result of the Pennsylvania legislature's reaction to the Great Labor Uprising of 1877, which had done millions of dollars' worth of damage to the property of the PRR and the city of Pittsburgh. Between 1878 and 1881, stimulated by the Pittsburgh business community, the legislature "completely overhauled the structure of the Pennsylvania militia" (Krause, 1992, pp. 134–35).

19. There is a caveat here: it must be borne in mind that it was mainly because of tariff barriers that shielded Carnegie Steel, and which it supported with money and lobbying efforts, that the Homestead mill was an economic entity in the first place.

20. In fact, Carnegie Steel was paying above-market wages at the time of the lockout and strike. Even with the reductions Carnegie and Frick wanted, wages at Homestead would have remained above the market standard.

7. EMPIRE BUILDER

1. Frick's role in this activity must not be omitted. For example, after the resolution of the lockout and strike at Homestead, Frick hired a man named P. R. Dillon to find ways to increase plant efficiency. Dillon adjusted the use of both machinery and men so that employment could be reduced by five hundred while output stayed the same. His efforts in all the Carnegie Steel works cut fifteen hundred jobs to produce the same output. As output expanded, men were rehired, and employment rose throughout the 1890s (Bridge, 1903, p. 296). As Warren (1996, p. 111) reminds us, "By the end of the 1890s, Carnegie Steel was the largest employer of labor in Pennsylvania, with the single exception of the Pennsylvania Railroad." Chapter 18 of Bridge's book also relates the efficiency that Frick brought to company management.

2. Misa (1995, p. 160) claims that it was Charles Schwab, not Carnegie or Frick, who pushed the deal that Oliver offered.

3. The next few paragraphs are based on Nevins (1953, vol. 2, pp. 248–66).

4. Part of the agreement that was later violated by Carnegie and Oliver required the Carnegie Steel Company to buy Mesabi ore solely from Rockefeller and to neither lease nor purchase any other sources of ore there. When these violations came to the attention of the Rockefeller interests, it led to intense negotiations. These culminated in twenty-eight contracts in 1900 to settle the disputed terms and compensate Rockefeller (Wall, 1970, pp. 609–11).

5. After the lockout and strike at Homestead in 1892, Schwab had replaced Potter as general superintendent at Homestead. At this point he was made a partner at 1/3 of 1 percent interest in Carnegie Steel. Schwab was promoted to the position of president on April 17, 1897, and his partnership interest increased to 1 percent. Within six months, it was upped to 3 percent (Hessen, 1975, pp. 68 and 74).

6. During the recession years, as it increased investment and expanded operations, Carnegie Steel's profit rose from $3 million in 1893 to $4 million in 1894, $5 million in 1895, $6 million in 1896, and $7 million in 1897 (Bridge, 1903, p. 295).

7. Krause (1992, p. 270–81) provides the sordid details of how Carnegie rigged bids and paid "commissions" in order to acquire the 144.48-acre City Poorhouse and Home for the Insane next to his Homestead plant for a little more than 70 percent of its estimated value. This was the land subsequently used for his armor plate mill, which was completed in 1892.

8. It must be mentioned that Carnegie may have claimed to be a pacifist, but he was not passive in securing this contract. Both his company and Bethlehem employed paid lobbyists and actively pursued the help of congressmen and "friends" in the Cleveland and Harrison administrations to secure contracts for armor plate and guns (in the case of Bethlehem) (Misa, 1995, p. 104). Carnegie was also adept at securing inside information on contract specifications in advance of their becoming public, as well as using political appointees, such as his old friend Secretary of State James G. Blaine, to secure foreign contracts (Wall, 1970, pp. 647–48).

9. Carnegie's objections to the production of guns had given way to the need for profits in the depressed 1890s, and, although he was now willing to bid for those contracts, he gave way in the face of his partners' argument in 1894 that the volume was not there (Wall, 1970, p. 653). The solution was found in an agreement with Bethlehem that Carnegie Steel would produce armor plate while Bethlehem produced armaments (Nasaw, 2006, p. 489).

10. In 1896, Secretary of the Navy Hilary A. Herbert had cost-of-production estimates made and was successful in reducing the price to $400 a ton, although the pooling arrangement was left undisturbed (Wall, 1970, p. 652).

11. Charles Schwab told Frick that the four men were employees hired during the Homestead lockout and strike and seemed disgruntled by the fact that the wages they received were less than expected. They also had a strict supervisor whom they disliked (Warren, 1996, pp. 153–56).

12. The following paragraphs are based primarily on Wall (1970, pp. 719–34), although other sources will be referenced as needed.

13. Gates got that nickname because he was known to bet for high stakes on anything (Hessen, 1975, p. 120).

14. Hendrick (1932, vol. 2, p. 79) gives the option signing date as April 24, 1899.

15. This note is reproduced as a photographic illustration in Bridge (1903, p. 320). Carnegie appeared before a congressional investigating committee in January 1912 and not only denied having been informed that Frick and Phipps had put up part of the $1,170,000 option money but also denied writing the note that promised to refund any money paid by his partners until a copy of it was put in front of him (Harvey, 1928, p. 206).

16. Nasaw (2006, p. 569) notes that Carnegie's copy of the minutes of that board meeting bears his handwritten inscription: "No Contract. Declaration of War."

17. Hendrick (1932, vol. 2, p. 93) claims that Frick intended to become a steel maker himself, while Bridge (1903, p. 324) says that Frick claimed that Carnegie had threatened to become a coke supplier. Presumably, this meant that Frick's purchase was defensive in nature.

18. Bridge (1903, p. 323) and Harvey (1928, p. 219) claim that the sale did not go through and Frick later sold the land to another party for $500,000 more than the price offered to Carnegie Steel. The minutes of the November 6 board meeting show unanimous approval of the sale (Wall, 1970, p. 739).

19. The full statement is reproduced from the minutes in Wall (1970, pp. 740–42).

20. Wall (1970, p. 753) relies on an interview with Frick's confidant, major stockholder, and former Carnegie, Phipps executive, John A. Walker, by Burton Hendrick on February 16, 1928, for this account of Frick's reaction and Carnegie's hurried retreat. As Nasaw (2006, pp.

574–75) points out, Hendrick's own account in his biography of Carnegie is based on a Carnegie memorandum that does not contain these words and portrays Carnegie as soberly perplexed by Frick's passion. Given Carnegie's propensity to portray his own actions in the strongest possible light, the Walker narrative seems more consonant with the characters of the two men. It is also important to remember that both Carnegie and Frick "possessed explosive tempers and were easily offended; they were accustomed to command, not to negotiate and eventually to compromise" (Hessen, 1975, p. 90).

21. Bridge (1903, pp. 337–38) says that Carnegie wrote the 1897 agreement so that its provisions extended to partners who were not indebted, but because his was the only signature on the document, it was invalid.

22. In a letter to Henry Phipps dated September 29, 1897, Carnegie says, "Did you not suggest that the power to expel should not apply to such as own their own interests, and hasn't your wish been granted?" (quoted in Harvey, 1928, p. 252).

23. As Hendrick (1932, vol. 2, pp. 69–70) points out, if one assumes a 6 percent rate, the $21 million return represents a one-year return on $350 million, and 6 percent was not an unusual interest rate for loan rates in financial markets at that time.

24. Harvey (1928, p. 254) quotes an old letter from Carnegie to Frick showing that Carnegie offered Abbott a 20 percent premium over book value for his stock.

25. As Temin (1964, p. 186) points out, stable prices over a substantial period is good evidence that a pool exists. Beginning with the 1890s, rail prices remained high during that decade, averaging $26 a ton, although it was not a decade of growth after the Panic of 1893. Following the incorporation of U.S. Steel, and beginning in 1902, steel rail prices became fixed at $28 a ton (Temin, 1964, table C15A). Misa (1995, p. 152) notes that they stayed at that price until 1915.

26. Carnegie's steel output in 1900 was 3 million tons; the output of his five major rivals was 3.5 million. His profits were $40 million; theirs were $48 million (Hessen, 1975, pp. 113–14).

27. The following two paragraphs are primarily based on Wall (1970, pp. 508–14), though also see Nasaw (2006, pp. 253–55).

28. The roadbed of the South Pennsylvania was not developed by the PRR but, fifty years later, developed by the state as the Pennsylvania Turnpike (Wall, 1970, p. 515).

29. Wall (1970, p. 789) shows a total of $480 million, but this includes the $40 million profit of 1900 and the same anticipated profit for 1901 among the assets to be sold.

30. As Hendrick (1932, vol. 2, p. 145) points out, Carnegie's demand for gold bonds for himself, his brother's widow, and his cousin Dod was made so that the three would be creditors of U.S. Steel rather than owners. Whatever the fortunes of the steel industry in the future, they would get their annual 5 percent and could find a ready market for sale of the bonds if desired. Since Carnegie planned to give away most of his fortune, it was now in a form easily transferable.

8. PHILANTHROPIST

1. The view that taxation should be used to provide libraries for "free" use by the general population in the United States was first codified into law by New York State in 1835. A state law was enacted that authorized "tax supported, free library service in each school district through a school district library to be used by the general public" (Bobinski, 1969, p. 4). The

view soon changed to the idea of the municipally owned, tax-supported, free public library. By 1896, the laws of twenty-nine states and Washington, D.C., authorized the socialization of library systems (Bobinski, 1969, p. 6).

2. Hendrick says that Carnegie believed "that public libraries were a state function, like the public school, and could become universal only when that principle was embedded in the popular consciousness" (1932, vol. 2, p. 202). Carnegie's purpose was to stimulate this by giving only the building and making the operating costs the responsibility of the locality. Again, according to Hendrick, "He sometimes referred to his library structures as 'bribes'" (1932, vol. 2, p. 203). It seems inconsistent that, as a boy, he went to a private school and used subscription libraries while, as an adult, he preferred to give to private universities and colleges while acting as one of the forces that eliminated subscription libraries.

3. Hendrick (1932, vol. 2, p. 200) says that only one-third of all the library buildings given by Carnegie bore his name.

4. Page number references given are taken from Wall's (1992) reprint in *The Andrew Carnegie Reader*.

5. The following draws primarily on Wall's (1984) enchanting history of Skibo before and during its ownership by the Carnegie family. As of this writing, the castle is owned and operated as "The Carnegie Club," a members-only hotel and country club. See www.carnegieclub.co.uk/index.html for exterior and interior views of this gorgeous old mansion.

6. According to Hendrick (1932, vol. 2, p. 88), Carnegie would tell visitors that the castle was "just a nice little present from Mr. Frick," referring, of course, to the $1,170,000 deposit that Carnegie had failed to return to Frick and Phipps after the option to sell Carnegie Steel to the Moore/Gates syndicate expired.

7. In its discussion of its own mission, the *Manual* (1919, p. 165) summarizes its specific purposes as investigating the causes of war and the practical solutions to its prevention, aiding the development of international law, educating the public in these matters, cultivating better relations between peoples of different nations, promoting peaceable methods for settling international disputes, and supporting institutions to accomplish these purposes. It seems an understatement to say that the period of world history that has followed the establishment of the Carnegie Endowment does not support much hope for its effectiveness. As one contemporary critic of the outlook for the project wrote one of the trustees, "He gives you ten millions of dollars to promote peace, every penny of which was the Dead Sea fruit of a war tariff . . . and he selects forty [men] pretty nearly every one of whom is a stand pat protectionist, and a red handed partisan of war upon every commercial nation . . . to spend millions for peace" (quoted in Wall, 1970, p. 900).

8. Hendrick (1932, vol. 2, p. 359) says that there were five hundred beneficiaries on the list, the total expenditure of which amounted to $250,000 annually.

9. In his autobiography, Carnegie says that large U.S. universities don't need the help as much as the smaller ones, especially small colleges like Dickenson College, Kenyon College, Western Reserve, Brown, Hamilton, Wells, Cooper Union, and Hampton and Tuskegee Institutes (Carnegie, 1920, p. 259). Hendrick says (1932, vol. 2, p. 261) that Carnegie gave libraries and science laboratories to small colleges to "level up mass intelligence." He also gave to trade schools like the Mechanics and Tradesmen's Institute in New York and the Franklin Institute in Boston.

10. This was the original foundation of what became the independent and nonprofit Teachers Insurance and Annuity Association–College Retirement Equities Fund (TIAA-CREF), now TIAA, and the dominant retirement savings vehicle for college and university professors in the United States.

11. Perhaps this was one of the fruits of his friendship with Herbert Spencer. According to Hendrick (1932, vol. 2, p. 282), Carnegie and Spencer were allies in their opposition to the South African War and the Philippine annexation. Spencer wrote Carnegie on January 9, 1900, that "all future progress depends upon the increasing predominance of industrialism over militancy. . . . The antagonism between the industrial and the militant types practically determines everything in civilization." Certainly, industrialism and general business activity prosper under conditions of peaceful relations and free trade among nations, while war means diversion of resources from the production of wealth to its destruction. Resources destroyed during war are resources lost to civilization forever. As a steel maker and manufacturer of armor plates for battleships, Carnegie would have stood to gain from a war with Chile. Yet, when President Harrison was inclined to go to war with that country, Carnegie strongly advised the president against it (Carnegie, 1920, pp. 350–52).

12. The building in Cartago was destroyed by earthquake in 1910, but Carnegie contributed the funds to build a replacement in San José, Costa Rica.

Bibliography

Barr, William T. 1947. *For a Web Begun: The Story of Dunfermline*. Edinburgh: Oliver and Boyd.

Bobinski, George S. 1969. *Carnegie Libraries: Their History and Impact on American Public Library Development*. Chicago: American Library Association.

Bostaph, Samuel. 2013. "Driving the Market Process: 'Alertness' versus Innovation and 'Creative Destruction.'" *Quarterly Journal of Austrian Economics* 16, no. 4, pp. 421–58.

Bridge, James Howard. 1903. *The Inside History of the Carnegie Steel Company: A Romance of Millions*. 3rd edition. New York: Aldine Book Company.

Burgess, George H., and Miles C. Kennedy. 1949. *Centennial History of the Pennsylvania Railroad Company: 1846–1946*. Philadelphia: Pennsylvania Railroad Company.

Burgoyne, Arthur G. 1893. *Homestead: A Complete History of the Struggle of July, 1892, Between the Carnegie Steel Company, Limited, and the Amalgamated Association of Iron and Steel Workers*. Pittsburgh.

Carnegie, Andrew. 1885. "The Road to Business Success: A Talk to Young Men." In Joseph Frazier Wall, ed. (1992), *The Andrew Carnegie Reader*. Pittsburgh: University of Pittsburgh Press.

Carnegie, Andrew. 1886a. "An Employer's View of the Labor Question." In Joseph Frazier Wall, ed. (1992), *The Andrew Carnegie Reader*. Pittsburgh: University of Pittsburgh Press.

Carnegie, Andrew. 1886b. "Results of the Labor Struggle." In Joseph Frazier Wall, ed. (1992), *The Andrew Carnegie Reader*. Pittsburgh: University of Pittsburgh Press.

Carnegie, Andrew. 1889. "The Gospel of Wealth." In Joseph Frazier Wall, ed. (1992), *The Andrew Carnegie Reader*. Pittsburgh: University of Pittsburgh Press.

Carnegie, Andrew. 1920. *Autobiography of Andrew Carnegie*. Boston: Houghton Mifflin.

Carnegie Endowment for International Peace. 1919. *A Manual of the Public Benefactions of Andrew Carnegie*. Washington, DC: Carnegie Endowment for International Peace.

Casson, Herbert N. 1907. *The Romance of Steel: The Story of a Thousand Millionaires*. New York: A. S. Barnes.

Demarest, David P., Jr., ed. 1992. *The River Ran Red: Homestead 1892*. Pittsburgh: University of Pittsburgh Press.

Flynn, John T. 1932. *God's Gold: The Story of Rockefeller and His Times*. New York: Harcourt Brace.

Foss, Nicolai J., and Peter G. Klein. 2012. *Organizing Entrepreneurial Judgment: A New Approach to the Firm*. Cambridge: Cambridge University Press.

Harvey, George. 1928. *Henry Clay Frick the Man*. New York: Charles Scribner's Sons.

Hendrick, Burton J. 1932. *The Life of Andrew Carnegie*. 2 vols. Garden City, NY: Doubleday, Doran.

Hessen, Robert. 1975. *Steel Titan: The Life of Charles M. Schwab*. New York: Oxford University Press.

Hughes, Jonathan. 1986. *The Vital Few: The Entrepreneur and American Economic Progress*. Expanded edition. New York: Oxford University Press.

Jackson, Robert W. 2001. *Rails Across the Mississippi: A History of the St. Louis Bridge*. Urbana and Chicago: University of Illinois Press.

Kirzner, Israel M. 1985. *Discovery and the Capitalist Process*. Chicago: University of Chicago Press.

Krause, Paul. 1992. *The Battle for Homestead, 1880–1892: Politics, Culture, and Steel*. Pittsburgh: University of Pittsburgh Press.

Lagemann, Ellen Condliffe. 1989. *The Politics of Knowledge: The Carnegie Corporation, Philanthropy, and Public Policy*. Middletown, CT: Wesleyan University Press.

Manual of the Public Benefactions of Andrew Carnegie. 1919. Washington, DC: Carnegie Endowment for International Peace.

Menger, Carl. [1871] 1950. *Principles of Economics*. Glencoe, IL: Free Press.

Misa, Thomas J. 1995. *A Nation of Steel: The Making of Modern America, 1865–1925*. Baltimore: Johns Hopkins University Press.

Mises, Ludwig von. 1960. *Epistemological Problems of Economics*. Princeton, NJ: D. Van Nostrand.

Mises, Ludwig von. 1963. *Human Action*. 3rd edition. New Haven, CT: Yale University Press.

Morris, Charles R. 2005. *The Tycoons: How Andrew Carnegie, John D. Rockefeller, Jay Gould, and J. P. Morgan Invented the American Supereconomy*. New York: Times Books.

Murray, Norman. 1978. *The Scottish Hand Loom Weavers, 1790–1850: A Social History*. Edinburgh: John Donald.

Nasaw, David. 2006. *Andrew Carnegie*. New York: Penguin Press.

Nevins, Allan. 1953. *Study in Power: John D. Rockefeller Industrialist and Philanthropist*. 2 vols. New York: Charles Scribner's Sons.

O'Driscoll, Gerald P., Jr. 1977. *Economics as a Coordination Problem: The Contributions of F.A. Hayek*. Kansas City, KS: Sheed Andrews and McMeel.

Reid, James D. 1886. *The Telegraph in America and Morse Memorial*. New York: John Polhemus.

Ridley, Matt. 2000. *Genome*. New York: Harper Perennial.

Schickel, Richard. 1960. *The World of Carnegie Hall*. New York: Julian Messner.

Schotter, H. W. 1927. *The Growth and Development of the Pennsylvania Railroad Company: A Review of the Charter and Annual Reports of the Pennsylvania Railroad Company 1846 to 1926, Inclusive*. Philadelphia: Allen, Lane & Scott.

Spencer, Herbert. [1851] 1995. *Social Statics*. New York: Robert Schalkenbach Foundation.

Spencer, Herbert. 1879. *The Data of Ethics*. New York: Hurst.

Spencer, Herbert. [1884] 1969. *The Man versus the State*. Caldwell, ID: Caxton Printers.

Stover, John F. 1997. *American Railroads*. 2nd edition. Chicago: University of Chicago Press.

Taussig, F. W. 1931. *The Tariff History of the United States*. 8th edition. New York: G.P. Putnam's Sons.

Temin, Peter. 1964. *Iron and Steel in Nineteenth-Century America: An Economic Inquiry*. Cambridge, MA: MIT Press.

Thomson, Daniel. 1903. *The Weaver's Craft: A History of the Weavers' Incorporation of Dunfermline.* Paisley: Alexander Gardner.

Wall, Joseph Frazier. 1970. *Andrew Carnegie.* New York: Oxford University Press.

Wall, Joseph Frazier. 1984. *Skibo.* New York: Oxford University Press.

Wall, Joseph Frazier, ed. 1992. *The Andrew Carnegie Reader.* Pittsburgh: University of Pittsburgh Press.

Warren, Kenneth. 1996. *Triumphant Capitalism: Henry Clay Frick and the Industrial Transformation of America.* Pittsburgh: University of Pittsburgh Press.

White, Richard. 2011. *Railroaded: The Transcontinentals and the Making of Modern America.* New York: W. W. Norton.

Index

Abbott, William, 78–79, 113, 151n24
Adams Express Company, 33–34
Aitkin, Andrew, 18, 22
Aitkin, Anne (Morrison), 22, 23, 24, 57
Allegheny Bessemer Steel Company, 67
Allegheny Portage Railroad, 28, 29–30
Amalgamated Association of Iron and
    Steel Workers (AAISW), 64, 78–79,
    81, 83, 86, 146n37, 147n1, 148n9
Anchor Cotton Mill, 1, 24
Anderson, James, 122
Atlantic and Ohio Telegraph Company, 25,
    26

Berkman, Alexander, 86
Bessemer process, 39–40, 48, 58–59, 68,
    100
Bessemer Steel Association, 59, 64, 67, 68
Bethlehem Iron Company, 104, 124,
    150n8–150n9
Botta, Anne Lynch, 49
Boyce, James, 89, 93
Brooks, David, 25, 26, 43
Burns, Robert, 18, 21

Cameron, Simon, 36, 140n3
Canmore, King Malcolm, 16
Cannon, Joe, 144n13
Cantillon, Richard, 6, 7
Carnegie, Andrew: on annexation of the
    Philippines, 131–132, 153n11; birth of,
15, 16; as bond salesman, 41–43; early
investments by, 33–34, 37–39, 43, 47;
education of, 21, 22, 25, 27, 29, 34–35,
36; as entrepreneur, 12, 39–40, 41, 62,
65, 67–68, 99–100, 125; on eugenics,
50; "Gospel of Wealth," 123–124, 125,
127; on heritage, 18; managerial
principles, 35, 59–62; marriage of,
71–72; personal character of, 1–2,
18–19, 22, 23, 26, 31, 32, 36, 42,
67–68, 108, 115, 141n16, 145n18,
146n26, 150n7; physical description of,
1, 23; residences of, 126–127; social
life of, 48–49, 70–71; on speculation,
139n2; on Spencer, 49–50, 54–55; on
tariffs, 46, 143n5; on unions, 74, 76; on
wages, 73–74, 78
Carnegie, Andrew (grandfather), 15, 17
Carnegie, James (uncle), 15
Carnegie, Kloman & Company, 38, 39, 40,
    56, 58, 62, 75, 76
Carnegie, Louise (Whitfield), 71–72, 106,
    124, 125–126
Carnegie, Lucy (sister-in-law), 119,
    151n30
Carnegie, Margaret (daughter), 106, 126
Carnegie, Margaret (mother), 16, 21, 22,
    24, 33, 34, 68, 70, 71, 141n9
Carnegie, McCandless & Company,
    56–57, 58

Carnegie, Phipps & Company, 65, 66,
    68–69, 77, 78, 80, 110, 148n7
Carnegie, Thomas (brother), 21, 34, 36, 38,
    39, 56, 57, 62, 68–69
Carnegie, William (father), 15, 16, 17, 18,
    20, 21, 22, 24, 56–57, 121–122
Carnegie (ship), 23, 130
"Carnegie Baths," 123
Carnegie Brothers & Company, Ltd.,
    62–63, 65, 67, 68–69, 76, 77, 78, 80,
    110
Carnegie Company, 113, 115–116, 119
Carnegie Corporation of New York, 129,
    132–133
Carnegie Dunfermline Trust, 130
Carnegie Endowment for International
    Peace, 127, 131
Carnegie Foundation for the Advancement
    of Teaching, 129, 152n10
"Carnegie Hall," 127–128
Carnegie Hero Fund Commission, 130,
    130–131
Carnegie Institute (Pittsburgh), 127
Carnegie Institution of Washington, 130
Carnegie Steel Company, Ltd., 69, 80, 99,
    100, 102–103, 104, 105, 107, 109,
    110–111, 112–113, 116, 149n1
Carnegie Trust for the Universities of
    Scotland, 128–129
Carnegie United Kingdom Trust, 132
Cassatt, Alexander J., 116
Central American Court of Justice, 130,
    131
Central Transportation Company. *See*
    Woodruff Sleeping Car Company
Chartist movement, 17
Church Peace Union, 130, 131
Clark, William, 64–65, 146n37
Cleveland, Grover, 105, 128
Coldstream Harbor Laboratory, 50
Coleman, William, 37, 56, 57, 58, 62
"College of Pattiemuir," 17
Columbia Oil Company, 37, 121
Credit Mobilier of America scandal, 140n1
Crowley, William, 25
Cyclops Iron Company, 38, 75

damask, 15, 16
Davenport, Charles, 50

Dodd process, 39
Drysdale, Charlotte, 22
Dunfermline Carnegie Library, 122

Eads, James, 41, 142n18
economic laws, character of, x
Edgar Thomson Steel Company, Ltd., 62,
    113
Exchange National Bank, 57, 58

Flowers, Roswell P., 108
Freedom Iron Company, 37, 39–40, 141n6
Frick, Henry Clay, 66–67, 69, 77, 78,
    79–80, 81–83, 86, 87–88, 97, 101, 103,
    105–106, 107–110, 111–115, 116, 133,
    148n5, 149n1, 150n11

Galton, Francis, 50
Gates, John W. ("Bet a Million"), 108,
    115, 117, 150n13
Gilchrist-Thomas, Sidney, 68
Glass, John P., 27
Graham, Sir John, 18

hand loom weaving: decline of, 19–21, 22;
    systems of manufacture, 15–16;
    working conditions, 17–18
Hay, John, 24–25
Henderson, Ailie Ferguson, 22
Hendrick, Burton, ix, 141n11, 144n14,
    150n14, 150n17, 151n23, 151n30,
    152n2–152n3, 152n6, 152n8, 153n11
history and theory, contrast between,
    11–12
Hogan, Andrew, 24
Hogan, Kitty (Morrison), 22, 23
Hogan, Thomas, 22, 23, 25
Holley, Alexander L., 57, 58–59, 64, 68,
    145n20
Homestead Strike, 69, 78–79, 80–90
Hughes, Jonathan R. T., ix
Huntington, Collis P., 140n1, 143n7

Illinois and St. Louis Bridge Company, 40,
    41, 142n17–142n18
"Iron Clad" agreements, 69, 110–111, 112,
    113

Jenney, William, 65, 146n38

Jevons, William Stanley, 93
Jones, Captain William R., 57, 63, 66, 69,
    75–78, 79, 122, 146n29, 146n35,
    147n41

Keppel, Frederick Paul, 133
Keystone Bridge Company, 38, 39, 40, 41,
    42, 56, 66
Keystone Telegraph Company, 43
Kipling, Rudyard, 128
Kirzner, Israel M.: capital theory, 9,
    147n41; entrepreneurship theory, 9–10,
    11, 96; following Mises, 8, 9; market
    process theory, 9
Kloman, Andrew, 37–38, 56, 57, 58, 62, 64
Kloman, Anthony, 37–38
Kloman and Phipps, 38, 75
Knight, Frank, 7–8, 11
Knights of Labor, 77, 78, 81, 87, 147n1
Krause, Paul, 89, 90, 147n1, 148n8,
    148n14–148n15, 149n16, 150n7

Lauder, George, 17, 18, 21
Lauder, George "Dod," Jr., 18, 80, 110,
    111, 119, 148n12, 151n30
Law, John, 6–7
law of association (comparative
    advantage), 142n2
Leishman, John, 106, 107, 113
Locke, John, 90–91, 96
Linville, Jacob, 38, 41

Macbeth, 16
Martin, Robert "Snuffy," 21, 22
Marx, Karl, 92
McCandless, David, 56–57, 58, 62
McCandless, Gardner, 62
McCargo, David, 25, 29, 36, 43
McCleary, William H., 83–84, 85, 86, 87
McKinley, William, 112, 143n5
Mechanics' and Apprentices' Library. *See*
    Anderson, James
Menger, Carl, 93–96
Merritt family, 100–102
Mill, John Stuart, 91–92, 93
Miller, Thomas, 25, 37–38
Misa, Thomas, 65, 66, 104, 146n38, 149n2
Mises, Ludwig von, 8–9, 11
"Mississippi Bubble," 6

Moore, James Hobart, 108, 114, 115
Moore, William H., 108, 114, 115
Morgan, J. P., 2, 61, 99, 115, 116, 117,
    118–119
Morgan, Junius S., 41, 58
Morrison, Thomas, 16–17, 21
Morrison, Thomas "Bailie," Jr., 17
Morrison, William, 22
Morse, Samuel F. B., 25

Nasaw, David, ix, 33, 89, 140n2, 144n17,
    147n2, 150n16, 150n20
New York Central Railroad, 33, 118–119
Nineteenth Century Club, 49

Oliver, Henry W., 25, 100, 101, 102, 103,
    104
O'Rielly, Henry, 26, 140n2

Pacific Railway acts, 47–48
Palace of Peace at The Hague, 130, 131
Pan American Union, 130, 131
Panic of 1873, 58, 99, 101, 146n32
Pearson, Karl, 50
Pennsylvania Railroad Company (PRR),
    28–30, 32, 33, 34–35, 36, 37, 38, 39,
    40–41, 42–43, 56, 59, 75, 86, 103, 116,
    118, 119, 124, 135, 140n3, 140n5,
    141n15
Phipps, Henry, 24, 141n9
Phipps, Henry, Jr., 37, 38, 39, 56, 57, 60,
    62, 68–69, 77, 80, 107–109, 110, 111,
    112, 114, 118, 141n9
Pinkerton Detective Agency, 78, 80, 82,
    84–86, 88, 89
Piper, John, 38
Piper and Shiffler, 38, 141n10
Pitcairn, Robert, 25, 29
Pittencrieff estate, 127, 130
Pittsburg Bessemer Steel Company, 64–65
Pontefract, John, 114
pooling agreements, 59, 67, 105, 115, 118,
    124, 145n25, 151n25
price level and income comparisons, 139n1
Pritchett, Henry Smith, 132
property rights, conflicting concepts of,
    88–90, 92–93, 96–97
protectionism, 45–47, 143n3
Pullman, George, 42, 43

Reform Acts of 1832, 17
Ricardo, David, 91, 92
Riddle, Anne Dike, 71
Robert the Bruce, 16, 18
Rockefeller, John D., 100, 102, 104, 107
Root, Elihu, 132

Schumpeter, Joseph A.: on capitalism, 10–11; critique of, 11; entrepreneurship theory, 10–12; and "ideal types," 11–12
Schwab, Charles, 61–62, 69, 79, 103, 104, 107, 109, 113, 116, 117, 118, 119, 146n29, 147n42, 149n2, 149n5, 150n11
Scott, John, 56, 57, 62
Scott, Thomas A., 1, 28–29, 30, 31–32, 33–36, 38, 40–41, 42–43, 56, 57, 58, 73, 74–75, 140n4
Seabreeze (yacht), 23, 126
Shiffler, Aaron, 38
Shinn, William P., 57, 59, 62, 113, 144n17
Skibo Castle, 72, 106, 108, 126
Smith, Adam: entrepreneurship theory, 7; labor theory, 91, 92; "Sympathy" theory, 51, 52
Spencer, Herbert: and Andrew Carnegie, 49–50, 54–55, 153n11; on government, 51–52, 54; on "law of equal freedom," 50–51, 53, 54; on "moral law of society," 50; on scientific ethics, 53; on social progress, 50, 52, 53; on welfare/philanthropy, 51–52
Stanford, Leland, 140n1
Stewart, David, 56, 57, 62
Stewart, Rebecca, 71
Stokes, Niles A., 32
Strobel, Charles L., 66
Sullivan, Louis, 65, 146n38
Sun City Forge Company, 141n6

Sutherland, Duke of, 126

tariff acts, 45, 46, 47, 57
Teachers Insurance and Annuity Association–College Retirement Equities Fund (TIAA-CREF). *See* Carnegie Foundation for the Advancement of Teaching
Thomson, John Edgar, 29, 30, 31, 33, 38, 40, 42, 43, 56, 57, 58
Tradesmans' and Mechanics' Library, 18, 122

U.S. Steel, 38, 119
Union Iron Mills, 38, 39, 58, 75, 147n2
Union Pacific Railroad, 42, 43, 48

value, theories of: labor theory, 90–93; marginal utility theory, 93–96; negation of labor theory, 94–97; value and price, 95–96
Vandevort, John W., 39, 62

Walker, John, 77, 111–112, 114, 150n20
Wall, Joseph Frazier, ix, 33, 68, 71, 88–89, 100, 104, 113, 129, 142n2, 143n6, 144n9, 144n17, 150n20, 151n29
Wallace, William, 18
Walras, Leon, 93
Washington, Booker T., 49, 128
Webb process, 39–40
Weber, Max, 11
Webster Literary Club, 49
White, Richard, 28, 35, 140n1, 140n4, 143n7
Wiscasset, 22, 23
Woodruff, T. T., 33, 128
Woodruff Sleeping Car Company, 33, 43

About the Author

Samuel Bostaph is emeritus professor of economics at the University of Dallas. He is the author of numerous scholarly publications on Carl Menger, William Stanley Jevons, Friedrich von Wieser, and other historical figures important to the development of the economic thought of the nineteenth century. Other historical figures on whom he has written at both scholarly and popular levels include Plato, St. Thomas More, Karl Marx, Joseph Schumpeter, Israel Kirzner, Lionel Robbins, Ayn Rand, and "Peace Mom" Cindy Sheehan. In 2005 he received the Lawrence A. Fertig Prize for the scholarly article published in the previous two years that best advanced economic science in the Austrian School tradition.